WORLD-BUILDING FOR WRITERS

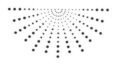

H.C. HARRINGTON

TITLES BY H.C. HARRINGTON

Fiction

Daughter of Havenglade

Black Dragon Deceivers

Blood Cauldron

Daughter of Dragons

The Inquisitor

Havenglade Tales

Nonfiction

World-Building for Writers

FOREWORD

Congratulations, by purchasing this book you've embarked on a quest that few people, and even many authors, will never pursue: becoming a master of world-building.

In your hand is a map of creative inspiration, good habits, and practical examples to ensure that you build a world that's fun and functional, that births heroes, cultivates epic tales, and inspires awe in readers.

If you're a heavy world-builder these chapters will inspire new inspiration. They will also make sure the world you are building has room for the story you're trying to tell. If you prefer a light touch, detail where you need it, and making up world-building on the fly, Harrington provides excellent rule of thumb for sketching out a vibrant and consistent world that grows as you need it.

Before I send you off on your quest I want to point out a couple of things this book does especially well. The first is identifying the sense of wonder and awe that draws readers to fantasy and science fiction. It's not just epic battles and massive dragons, but also the small details: the girl lost in the forest who finds a small cave with a tiny dragon; the old wizard hunched over a table, crafting mysterious potions with a glowing crystal; the young hero hiding out in the woods behind a sleepy fishing village.

Truly mastering world-building is about more than just cool characters with epic backstories or realistic and complicated settings. Though you'll find plenty of those here. It's also about finding the story at the intersection of those things. You will notice almost never in this book does a tidbit of world-building get suggested without a corresponding scrap of story to go along with it.

In a lot of ways, a nonfiction book about normal people in the modern day is only as real as it is believable or as real as the mark it makes on the mind of the reader. This is why the most memorable world history books are the ones that tell stories and paint a picture of their subjects as dramatic characters. If the measure of a book's importance, then, is based off of the lessons we can learn and the truths it teaches, stories about spaceships and dragons become far more important than we ever realized. And making sure that the worlds that we tell the stories in are believable and inspiring is the best way to discover real truth and meaning behind every fantastic tale.

-Dustin Porta
April 2021

CHAPTER ONE

Why Write a Book on World-Building?

I asked myself this very question many times while I worked on the outline for this book. The answer came about rather unexpectedly. As writers, you might understand the circumstances that brought me to this place.

Like many, I'd grown disillusioned with the myriad of social media platforms that seem to play greater and greater roles in our lives—especially the lives of us writers! Websites like Facebook had become extremely toxic and polarizing. I often found my friends and family arguing, with little thought of courtesy or decorum, about nearly any topic that came up—and don't even get me started on politics.

It was almost enough to make me want to build a new world right then and there, just to escape from the absurdity of the one I was living in. Until that time—and even now, I guess—I'd put little time into building my author presence online. With Twitter and, to some extent, KBoards that soon changed.

As I networked with more writers, both traditionally published and independent, I became really excited about what was going on within the online writing community. Writers were largely positive and supportive, posting many topics related to craft and marketing, which helped me keep my mind on the goals I had set. People often openly asked for advice with whatever problems they faced in their writing or publishing process.

As my newsfeed began to fill with more and more writer-related content, I started to enjoy using social media again. People showed each other respect and seemed eager to prop one another up in the spirit of our shared craft. What's more, if I came across someone too negative, I could simply unfollow them. Things were looking up for me and the new author friendships I was forming online.

Now, you might be wondering how this relates to world-building. Well, I started gravitating towards social media and writer's forums for topics about writing craft. Often, it was to help improve my own skills, to gain motivation, or merely to see where others were on their writing journeys, but more and more I found myself spending time discussing world-building with other fantasy and science-fiction writers. There was a tremendous amount of knowledge being shared—and there still is. I recommend every writer build up a social media presence that's centered on the writing community before using that presence to promote their work to readers, but you do you.

I came across many writers who were excited about building the worlds for their stories. There were often open-ended questions being asked, and many writers mentioned the lack of comprehensive web resources on the subject. There is a scattering of blog posts and several books written on world-building, but writers were either failing to connect with the content or having trouble implementing the advice given, which was often generic and felt rushed.

I found myself stepping in to offer a tip here and there, and in the process, started to realize, *I might have more to share on this subject than I thought.* Even as the idea crossed my mind, I didn't think it was my place to give that sort of advice, seeing as how I was still finishing up my first fantasy series. The more I thought about it, though, the more I noticed other writers were finding my advice useful and actionable, and writers were asking me lots of follow-up questions privately.

I started to wonder why more writers hadn't written about the subject of world-building. I scoured through Amazon, turned over every craft book in several massive libraries, and put Google to work, all in the name of finding first-class, world-building advice. While I did find amazing nuggets of information, it was scattered throughout so many blog posts and random chapters spread across many craft books that I began to realize why so many authors were struggling with the learning process.

With this knowledge, I again became introspective. I asked myself: *Well, how did you learn about world-building? Why do you feel confident you can help writers get through this part of the writing process?* Those were important questions I needed to reflect on if I wanted to create the kind of writing resource that would *actually* help, and not just another book collecting dust on some writer's desk.

I thought everyone played Dungeons and Dragons.

I had some socially rough years from the time around my parents getting divorced—I was around eight years old if memory serves—up until my sophomore year of high school. I was moving back and forth between two disruptive households and many different schools, shuffling through friends, classes, and teachers, not really able to find my place living in a single-parent household where I was often left to my own devices. I was sometimes too shy and too new to break into the cultivated social groups of adolescent life.

To put it another way, I was a nerd. To make matters worse, I wasn't even a nerd who got good grades. Double ouch! Why am I talking about this awkward part of my childhood? Well, that's where my experience with world-building first began. From a young age, I read a variety of books, even some Stephen King novels that were *way* too adult for me, but no one had told me not to read them.

I was most attracted to fantasy and sci-fi, though. Early on, I read *The Hobbit, The Chronicles of Narnia* series by C.S. Lewis, and Piers Anthony's humorous takes on the fantasy genre like *A Spell for Chameleon* and *Ogre, Ogre*, but I was really caught up in books from the *Dragonlance* series. I may have been reading *Dragons of Winter Night* when I first realized the rich worlds created through fantasy fiction appealed to me. The quests were great fun. I followed along as the characters trialed toward becoming *Heroes of the Lance*. They traveled to far-off amazing places in that trilogy, like the island of Southern Ergoth and the Icewall Glacier, meeting elves, dragons, and all manner of fantastic creatures along the way.

My first real crack at world-building came when I roamed the aisles of a local bookstore. The section near the fantasy novels was full of different kinds of books: books for games, supplemental materials to help groups play and prepare *Dungeons and Dragons* sessions, book-sets with full campaigns one could play with friends.

I didn't really know what I was looking at back then, but staring back at me was a large hardcover book with a menacing fighter on the cover—if memory serves. It was the *D&D Player's Handbook*. I took this book home and spent weeks going through every little detail of how to build a world in D&D. What were the different races? We had humans, elves, halflings, dwarves—and so many other choices. The classes were wonderful things like wizards, thieves, rogues, bards, and warriors. There were even alignments for your character's personality and morality. Would your character be a goody two-shoes Lawful Good Paladin or a Chaotic Evil Rogue?

These alignments have gone full meme status in our present day, but back then, they were little-known-to-the-outside-world ways to define the way you would play your character. From True Neutral, and Lawfully Evil, to Neutral Good, and other such varieties that could be chosen at your whim. It was fascinating to me that such games were being played by groups of friends all over the world. It seemed complex and interesting. I set out to learn more by printing copies of the player sheets and rolling my "stats". Basically, the dice gave you options on how powerful, wise, charismatic, etc. your character could start out as. Once I had it all down, I realized if I wanted to ever play this game, I'd need to learn how to set up a campaign or adventure.

For Christmas or maybe for my birthday, I acquired *The Dungeon Master's Guide* and *The Monstrous Compendium*. With all this new world-building knowledge at my disposal, I set about creating my own campaign. Making the creative decisions felt fantastic, even though I mostly just selected options from what I read in the books.

I went to the stationery store and purchased some graphing paper —the kind that is a full page of small boxes—and used those as maps for my adventures. One shaded-in box would represent a peasant's hovel, two might be a small shop, four shaded in a square shape might be a large shop. I created a castle, walls, a moat, different structures within the castle. I was having tons of fun spending a lot of time by myself, building up my own adventures—which was also something I enjoyed doing.

The time came to present this quest to the few friends I had wherever I was those months—remember I was moved around a lot. We played the quest, but about halfway through, my two friends wanted to play *F-Zero* on the Super Nintendo. I couldn't believe they could even be thinking of a racing game we'd already played countless times. Apparently, they weren't as immersed in my fantasy world as I was. On top of that, I probably made loads of mistakes playing D&D, since we were just kids at the time with no experienced players to direct us.

Not long after, I moved again. New school, new classmates, new home. I still had all my notes, maps, and character sheets, but I found no one in the new city to play the game with, and so the books found their way onto a shelf where they collected dust for some time.

In high school, I moved back with my mother after only a couple of months, ruining my first semester. Once I started at the new school, I found it difficult to fit in. In class, I got picked on for being a quiet loner with less than fashionable clothing. Mercifully, at the end of the year, I moved yet again. At my third high school, things went smoother. I started playing football, joined the track-

and-field team, made friends, started finding girlfriends. I enjoyed high school, for a change. Fantasy world-building went on the back-burner. I even started to believe the hype that "only nerds" played games like that.

When I was a kid scouring through my player's handbook, I had thought everyone would eventually play D&D. It just seemed too interesting an activity for anyone to not want to take part in. Boy, was I wrong!

Throughout the years, until the magic moment when I decided to try my hand at writing, I read constantly. Just to give you some insight into what I read during that time: Michael Crichton books like *Jurassic Park, Sphere,* and *Rising Sun*; Stephen King books such as *The Stand, The Shining,* and *Pet Semetary*; Tolkien's *The Hobbit*; a lot of *Choose Your Own Adventure* books; and sci-fi like *Dune, Ender's Game,* and *The Foundation* series.

As I eventually grinded through college and finished my degree in anthropology and history, I ended up studying abroad in China—which is a story for another time. I taught English in Taipei, and for whatever reason, perhaps again moving to a new place where I didn't really know anyone, I got back into the idea of world-building.

I wanted to write a story.

I had never done anything creative enough growing up. I had never taken music classes, though I did have a decent singing voice and was in the school choir in middle school. I never showed much promise at art, and perhaps it nagged at me over the years—subconsciously, of course, as I never sat down and thought *I should try to be creative.* I was in a bookstore in Taipei one day, where I found myself looking at the few English books available on writing. I bought one that was fairly useless—I won't name the title here—but I quickly found a better book that explained a lot of the basics about being a writer.

At the time, this was strictly a hobby. I had never once thought about selling a story and would have had no confidence to do so in those early days. I picked up enough of the basics, though, and worked up the confidence to start putting pen to paper and writing little shorts. Awful little stories with no flow, poor pacing, hard-to-understand locations and characters.

It was a mess . . . but I was learning.

When I was back stateside, I opened the boxes and dusted off all those old D&D books, character sheets, and graphing-paper maps I had made as a child. It felt like there was something more for me to discover. It was more than just a game. Could I be creative through world-building and storytelling? I wasn't so sure.

I didn't even know what kind of story I wanted to write. My first attempt at writing was a zombie apocalypse story that I eventually shelved and left on an old laptop, which I ended up selling. Lost to the world—probably for the best.

I spent a lot of time trying to figure out what kind of story might work best. Back in Taipei, I was in my classroom after class, chatting with a student. I asked her what kind of story I should write, and she said, "A story with a girl who saves the world." The idea stuck with me. Although it probably didn't materialize the way in which my student had imagined, her answer led me down the path to writing my first book, *Daughter of Havenglade*, which became a modestly successful jumpstart for my writing career.

I knew right then that I would write a fantasy quest in the tradition of what I had learned from reading the works of Joseph Campbell and the hero's journey—books like *The Hero with a Thousand Faces*, *The Power of Myth*, and his *Masks of God* series. I had also wanted it to be an almost naïve tale harking back to the stories of my youth, where magic was mysterious, and the world was epic in scale. This led me deeper into world-building. I hadn't read *The Lord of the Rings* trilogy at that point—only *The Hobbit*. I worked my way through the trilogy and on to George R. R. Martin's *A Song of Ice and Fire* series. I learned a great deal about world-building from those two fantastic series, and I set out to become a writer.

I'll spare you that story because I think I've given enough of a personal biography for you to understand my connection to what this book seeks to accomplish—helping writers in whatever world-building undertaking they may be struggling with.

I'm genuinely excited to write this book. Knowing I've contributed positively to the writing community would be an amazing feeling, especially if my book finds itself in the hands of young indie writers who are struggling with their journey.

Enjoy!

—H.C. Harrington
April 2020

CHAPTER 2

World-Building For People Who Don't Want To World-Build

So, you don't like world-building? I won't judge you. I'm here to help! Many writers have little time and energy to spend on their craft as it is—I know the feeling. Occasionally, a writer friend will comment on how difficult it is to balance life with a writing career. How can they justify spending the precious little creative time they have thinking about geography, made-up histories, constructed languages, and everything else entailed in creating realistic worlds?

I'm here to walk you through the basics, and not without a myriad of examples from some of the most beloved world-builders in the fantasy and science-fiction pantheon. We will explore examples from literature, television, graphic novels, computer games, and the silver screen—to name but a few.

After journeying with me through this book, I hope you'll have been introduced to more than enough creative elements to present a believable world to your readers. One of the best tricks of world-building an author can learn is to give the reader a feeling that something is hiding around every corner, and that the world continues vibrantly off the page.

I'm going to give you a healthy portion of easy-to-follow examples that you can feel free to use some variation of in your own stories, if they fit. Just be sure to add a unique element to them. If you plug in a few minor variations, you'll have something of your own without scouring many pages of research, hoping to get things right.

Most readers fall into that camp.

They are most interested in reading the story. They want to follow the characters as they tackle the challenges that face them. But—and this is a big but—they need to believe in the world through which the characters are traveling, at least enough to suspend disbelief, which is a test each writer must overcome to win over the willing reader. Like Agent Fox Muller from the *X-Files*, they want to believe!

Your world might be full of dragons and magic, but if it feels too vague or bland, your readers will have a harder time settling into your story.

W hy should I worry about world-building? you might be asking.

That's a great question, one I certainly seek to answer with this book. I've heard many writers say something along the lines of: "I don't want to waste my time writing about things that barely affect the plot or the characters. I don't have enough time for writing as it is."

I completely understand that mindset.

If you are writing fantasy in the genre of Tolkien or George R.R. Martin or writing sci-fi in the genre of Heinlein or Orson Scott-Card, you need to be aware that these works aren't only great stories, they are world-building masterpieces. Tolkien created entire constructed languages—the Elvish dialects like Quenya and Common Telerin—when it was unheard of and little to no resources available to take on such daunting tasks. Of course, Tolkien was a trained philologist, so that certainly helped. But remember how cool Elvish sounded in those blockbuster *The Lord of the Rings* movies or how amazing the script of Tengwar looked?

More than once, Tolkien mentioned that the Middle-earth stories, including *The Lord of the Rings*, grew out of his constructed languages. Talk about some hardcore world-building!

None of us grew up in a medieval castle or during pre-scientific times. That makes it all the more challenging to create the worlds that resemble—in many ways—the technological levels and habits of those times. It's very difficult to write believable fantasy if the characters all act like post-modernist teenagers, but believe me, it's challenging to remove the modern ticks from our writing. I cringe at how many "Yeahs" and "okays" I had to edit out of my first manuscript. I did learn better, though, I promise.

If you are, at the very least, aware of the seminal cultural historical events that drive the behavior and shape the society you are writing about, you can more easily suspend the reader's disbelief about your fantasy world, allowing them to soak up the plot and the characters.

In other words, if the reader believes you when you write about wagons and whetstones, they will buy into your dragons and wizards, because after all, that's what they signed up for when they picked up your fantasy story.

Writing Tip: If you make the mundane aspects of your story believable, the readers will willingly accept the magical aspects. After all, they purchased a fantasy novel, not a scientific textbook.

A unique idiom, a clever song verse, or an interesting historical reference will add an organic sense of depth to your story, turning your story's world into an interesting aspect of the plot in its own right.

Hark back to *A Game of Thrones* and the words of House Stark: *Winter is coming.* Or the words of House Greyjoy: *What is dead may never die.* These basic phrases keep coming back up in the story whenever their meanings are required as a sense of protection and identity for the characters, and it ties in marvelously with the story to enhance character and plot. Perhaps the most famous song in fantasy epics is *Far Over the Misty Mountain Cold* from *The Hobbit.* It's a very minor part of the story, but it really gives you a sense of what the dwarves hold important in their racial and cultural identity.

A question one might ask is: "How do I know if and where I should add this sort of element into my world-building?"

H ere are a few questions to consider that will help you decide:

1) Would the scene be better without it? If the answer is yes, don't add it.

2) Does the song or idiom stand on its own? If it does, then you probably have something special that will enhance your world.

3) What purpose does it serve the story? If you can identify a reason to justify it, it's likely a good fit.

4) Is it something that *works* with the characters in the story? Would your gruff, rogue, blood elf sing a love song? Perhaps, just make sure it's right for the moment.

In Phillip K. Dick's *Do Androids Dream of Electric Sheep?*—a sci-fi classic and the source material for *Blade Runner*—the concept of *kipple* is such a simple yet interesting aspect of Dick's world-building. Kipple is a useless object like a used matchbook, an empty soda can, an orange peel, or anything else that seems to multiply and take over, especially in our home, if we get too lazy. Kipple can take over one's home or city as useless objects pile up. It's a cool use of a word to add depth and provide a view into the thoughts of Dick's character and worldview.

In short, I've provided fledgling world-builders with clear examples of how simple world-building choices can add depth and value to their stories. After reading through these examples and the thought process behind them, I'm sure writers will be able to incorporate unique details into their own world-building.

Some writers just need the basics and that's what the first half of this discussion is centered on.

CHAPTER 3

How to Create a World

L et's get started!

The bare minimum required of your fictional world is an environment and a society.

Choose an environment in which the story will take place. I like to think of these things in the form of what-if questions. Take Frank Herbert's Science Fiction classic Dune for example. What if I wrote a story that took place on a barren desert planet? At first it sounds too simplistic to make an entire planet consisting of an environment of dune-filled deserts, but as is often the case, restrictions breed creativity. Once you have the idea of a desert planet there needs to be a pretty good reason for a story to take place there, a reason for people to want to live there among a galactic kingdom including many worlds, and a reason for a reader to be drawn in and interested. I'll greatly simplify the work of Herbert to break things down, essentially, the reason a desert planet is interesting enough is because there is something everyone wants there. A common theme in world-building is to take something undesirable and give it a reason to be desirable.

No one would ever pay attention to the planet Arrakis if not for that all-important spice which fueled many products throughout the empire. So we have a desert planet, and an important resource, now we need characters!

Herbert wanted Arrakis to be part of a huge space fiefdom, but there's no reason the rulers of the galaxy would have for living on such a barren world. They should live somewhere more glamorous, more beautiful, in a land far away. Though, he realized that the characters inhabiting this world needed to be important in some way. Well, why not have the planet run by a powerful royal family? Make it a prestigious honor to look after the barren spice planet, and send a new family to take over the work. Enter House Atreides. And this is where your skills as a story-teller come into play. Because with geography, setting, and character a writer can start crafting a plot, character tensions, setting, theme, and all of the other good stuff that goes along with it.

Another noteworthy example from the world of Fantasy is Ursula K. Le Guin's amazing The Left Hand of Darkness. The story takes place on the always winter planet of Gethen. Le Guin blends the environment and creates a fascinating race of people whose sex changes based on cycles. They choose partners based on their current sex. Saying this concept is unique is akin to saying pizza is a popular choice on game night with the boys. The world is extreme in that it only has one environment, but the author weaves world-building elements around this and her race of beings to create an engrossing world that readers have no problem falling into.

You could also use a world like ours with familiar environments so that readers can focus directly on the story. In my first novel, Daughter of Havenglade, I made a conscious choice not to depart far from traditional Fantasy in terms of the environments because I wanted to present my version of the timeless quest or hero's journey. It was my first major story—50,000+ words—and I wanted it to fit in well with the typical tropes of the genre as I wasn't as confident to step out too far from convention back in those days. Gradur Castle is the epicenter of Havenglade and is surrounded by Havenglade City. It rests in a picturesque valley with snow-capped mountains to the west, and rolling farmland, and grasses to the north, east, and south. Many of the characters are from valley villages. There is a rich port city—that doesn't show up in the series though it's referenced enough to build a feeling about it—and finally the threat comes from the harsh badlands to the east. It's really quite basic, and most of my world-building takes place after the geographic features are put in place.

Perhaps your protagonist lives in an isolated mountain village and has only heard fanciful stories of the outside world. The readers might deeply enjoy discovering it with her as she ventures out of the known and comfortable and into the unknown abyss. Could you present a believable mountain village? With a bit of thought I believe any writer could.

How do they subsist in the mountains? No mining please, unless you have a really interesting new angle. It's overdone in fantasy and requires a lot of logistics in practice to mine in the mountains. How about shepherds tending mountain goats or sheep in lush alpine meadows? They bring their animals up during the summer to graze the otherwise untouched foliage before returning to lower elevations as the snow and deathly cold returns to the high mountain peaks. This naturally leads us to skills that would be necessary to take care of livestock, transport animals, identify weather patterns, survive in potentially harsh environments, etc.

Many writers still haven't realized that a little world-building naturally leads to setting, theme, and character sculpting. You could have a young shepherd who wishes for a life outside of the isolated mountain village he's been around his whole life. Hunters returning one day tell tales of a caravan of traders passing through the basin with many exotic goods and strange clothing. Could this be the chance our young shepherd has been waiting for to go out on an adventure? Probably...especially since his father is a drunk who beats and criticizes him to the breaking point. Built-in conflict is around every corner when you spend a few moments to develop your world-building.

Pick a random geographical feature as an exercise. How about a waterfall? Maybe there is a system of caves behind it leading to... well that's for you to decide. Or maybe the waterfall is the place where a young unicorn comes to drink every morning and a curious elven princess seeks to tame the beautiful and mysterious wild creature.

Maybe your planet feels like the beloved moon of Endor from the Star Wars Universe. A place of endless forest and hints of only the most basic of civilizations. In a world of massive trees safety comes from living off of the ground. The tree houses on Endor are some of the more memorable aspects of Star Wars's world-building in my estimation. Watch those scenes again in the Return of the Jedi. You feel like you are in a fleshed out world even though it's just a forest moon with tree houses and puppet-like critters. Hollywood loves these type of "high-concept" premises. A famous example is the box-office flop— but greatly hyped movie Waterworld directed by Kevin Reynolds. He took the idea of climate change and turned it into a concept. What if the earth was completely covered in water? And then it became a full-fledged premise. What if the secrets to the location of the fabled "dryland" was hidden in plain-sight on the tattoo of a young girl and only one man could protect her from the evil Smoker pirates who will stop at nothing to find her?

This is literally a story about a water environment to the extreme. So what do people do? Well they need to live on man-made structures and know how to fish or catch birds. Humanity is fragmented by necessity. Factions are the order of the day. Might makes right. Mad Max at sea if you will. The basic world-building is simplistic. The concept is ambitious and the story is fast-paced. We can argue about the execution of the movie and why it ultimately failed, but its world-building will be remembered for years to come because of its ambitious and interesting implications and the inherent possibilities it had to offer.

Writing Tip: You don't absolutely need a unique environment or geography for your story as long as you meet the minimums for believability and give the readers a few solid details that draw them in.

"**W**hat about the city or surroundings that the main characters will be living in or traveling through? Don't I need to make a super realistic town or city down to the street names, detailed maps of where each structure is located, and who works or lives there?"

This is the type of question that comes up sometimes in writing craft forums or in some of our "tweet conferences" on twitter within the #writingcommunity.

Well, the short answer is no. If the story is moving quickly and the plot is intriguing you can go light on the world-building, but you can make it memorable with very little effort on your part.

In the third and fourth books of my Daughter of Havenglade series titled Blood Cauldron and Daughter of Dragons respectively, my merry band of travelers spent a decent amount of time stopping off in small villages and roadside inns on their quest. I didn't want to take a lot of time making loads of details for small villages that our travelers would barely remember themselves, let alone the readers, but one way I added some flavor to the story was to spend a bit of time on the names for the inns and taverns and to make some of the people they deal with have interesting or distinct dialogue. Some villages were surrounded by a basic wooden palisade. I added a suspicious gatekeeper who questions the travelers as they enter the village. I recommend something like a chatty barkeep or serving gal who might just drop some local gossip on them that changes everything. We could throw in the feelings the characters have about the food and drink they're served or their observations about the locals and travelers around them.

Writing Tip: Take something that would normally be undesirable and make it desirable like Frank Herbert did with his desert planet in Dune. Or do the opposite, take something desirable and flip it on its head to make it undesirable under certain circumstances. What if the young prince feels like the castle he lives in is more prison than paradise? This is not only true of world-building but is a useful method for developing the themes of your story as well.

CHAPTER 4

Not Thinking About Infrastructure?

"Infrastructure? I'm a writer, not an engineer."

The very word sounds boring enough to elicit a yawn. The idea of building the structures that make up the realm your citizens live in might not sound interesting, but believe me, it absolutely is! The infrastructure you create will give your world a sense of realism your readers can settle into. It doesn't need to be tedious or difficult to create. And no, you don't need to be an architect or an engineer to create realistic structures in your world.

One of the simplest examples I can think of is the Kingsroad in George R.R. Martin's *A Song of Ice and Fire* series. The concept is not unique or new. It's a composite of roads made from kingdoms throughout history. Sometimes, it serves the purpose of a continental Silk Road of sorts where citizens can travel from the far reaches of the north to King's Landing, and even all the way down to exotic Dorne in the far south of Westeros. The Latin *mille viae ducunt homines per saecula Romam,* "A thousand roads lead me forever to Rome" or the more modern English idiom, "All roads lead to Rome". It's just a road, but in a medieval world, having a road like that is a *big* deal. We take for granted how easy it is to get around on our endless streets and freeways but think about the world you are creating. If it's a medieval fantasy setting, it would be difficult to get around without a reliable road. But who will make one? Is it just going to be created by the hooves of thousands of horses as they make countless trips to a trade hub? That's perfectly fine, but it's a nice detail to use in your story.

I n another example from *ASOIAF*, Martin uses the Kingsroad as a location for many of his scenes. It's a pretty simple use of location but knowing that it's the main road linking the important points across the Seven Kingdoms, we can assume there might be chances for conflict along the road. Robbers, rapists, trade caravans, knights of an enemy's bannermen, orphans moving along looking for a new start in a never-before-visited city, or a wronged peasant traveling to the castle to air his grievances to the king. The sky is the limit, and the road is long. The Kingsroad is even used effectively in the story when the characters aren't even near it. Characters wanting to keep from being seen by the wrong folks steer clear of the Kingsroad on multiple occasions throughout the series. In that sense, the Kingsroad becomes something to avoid—an actual danger.

In my fantasy mystery adventure, *The Inquisitor*, I make the location a central part of the plot by linking backstory and theme with the various important aspects of the location. The city of Pax Grati—which is only mentioned in my *Daughter of Havenglade* series, never visited by the reader until this standalone story— gets the full treatment because I felt it had so much to offer me in terms of world-building, and I knew that would help me write the plot, theme, and characters. It's the richest city in the kingdom, even richer than the capital city of Havenglade itself. It's also the major port linking trade along the Sea of Epiphany. There's a lot of work to be found on the docks and on the various ships that frequent the harbor, for those who want it. Many of the nobles have earned their riches through financing trade voyages, establishing import/export businesses, and by taking advantage of the cheap and uneducated laborers coming from the countryside looking for work.

Tying the city of Pax Grati's identity to the port harbor didn't require a lot of contemplation. It was a build-up from the initial idea. As I wrote *The Inquisitor*, ideas popped into my head about how I could exploit the existing aspects of the port harbor, and I'd make notes so I could incorporate those ideas into the plot later.

Another famous example of simple infrastructure comes from J.R.R. Tolkien's world of Middle-earth. I could, of course, take many examples, and I do give a few more throughout this book, but let's start with something from the Shire. The Shire is a pleasant, sleepy, little village, home to several large families of hobbits. They tend their gardens and seem to live a relaxing life without many stressors. It's a great place to start a story. It eases the reader into the normalcy of daily life for the characters before everything changes. Hobbit-holes, otherwise known as Smials, are those round-doored little houses built into the side of hills all throughout the Shire. They, of course, draw attention to the relative smallness of the hobbits themselves, but also give a distinct feeling that these creatures are connected to the natural world around them. They live in houses that are still recognizable to us humans, but aren't they just fancy burrows? An advanced hole? That's up to the reader to decide, but they certainly contrast with the huge castles and simple hovels we see humans inhabiting.

As Tolkien developed the hobbits, I'm sure the hobbit-holes were detailed right along with them. The Shire, the hobbit-holes, and some of the most fondly remembered world-building elements of *The Hobbit* and *The Lord of the Rings* trilogy come down to a masterful weaving together of theme, plot, characters, and world-building.

You could devise a clock tower with a mysterious history and strange architecture in the middle of your capital city, and then weave it into a scene or two. Perhaps something sinister happened in the bell tower long ago? A ghost that comes out as the clock chimes midnight? Or you could have a sacred river running through the heart of the protagonist's hometown. Perhaps the city upstream is polluting the river with waste and debris, and when it reaches the town, the water is filthy and almost worthless to the protagonist and his neighbors. This might prompt a story—a trip to the city to try and put a stop to the desecration of the river. But wait, how is a river infrastructure? Isn't that part of geography and environment? Yes, it is, but it's only a river until the village is built around it and the importance of it is created for a community of people. It's a part of their lives and their culture, which is much different than a river that exists but has no significance to the characters or the story.

Writing Tip: Think about infrastructure and how it can enhance your story. Even something as simple as a road or a marketplace can add considerable depth to the believability of your locations. It might even inspire creative nuance in your plot, themes, and characters.

CHAPTER 5

One Dimensional Races

I spend a lot of time reading fantasy and science fiction. The world-building aspect I see least taken advantage of in the current market seems to be the development of non-human races or species. Especially in the indie writing community, you'll see many exact copies of races from *The Lord of the Rings.*

Why are dwarves always bearded miners—invariably male because it's much harder to sexualize them—who live underground? You might be saying, "But wait, *that's* what dwarves *are.*" No, that's what *Tolkien's* dwarves are, but you are allowed to make your dwarves whichever way you like, or even create something you've never seen done before. You don't even need to call them dwarves. Don't automatically fall into the habit of using orcs, goblins, elves, halflings, and the rest of the Tolkien-inspired races. Try to carve out some unique space for your own creatures whenever possible.

I was guilty of this same mistake with my first series. In *Daughter of Havenglade*, which started out as an evening hobby to unwind after work, I knew that I knew close to nothing about the art or business of writing. I just wanted to create a story that reminded me of the classic fantasies from my childhood, which tended to follow what is now sometimes referred to as noble bright fantasy. I created a race of humanoids that were more or less big orcs called bandi. I did very little to build their distinct characteristics early on, beyond setting them in the badlands of my world and giving them regional warlords that I thought would make them seem barbaric and menacing. I even gave them green scaly skin like all the other derivative baddies! Ugh . . . If I were to start that story over from the beginning, the bandi would certainly be much different. I'd give them more of that unique space I just mentioned. I'd give them unique cultural practices and beliefs that would end up playing a part in the conflicts of the series and not just use them as arrow fodder for the more important characters. They don't hurt the story, but they certainly aren't doing me any favors, considering how many similar flavors of orcs and goblins we already have in fantasy.

I also included elves in *Daughter of Havenglade*, but here I was more careful to differentiate them from the elves we are used to encountering in other stories. Being elves, they are still derivative of previous iterations in much of their appearance, but I hope I've made them different enough that they stand on their own merits. The elves in *Daughter of Havenglade* are horse masters who live on the plains to the northeast of Havenglade, not the forest archers we are used to from *The Lord of the Rings* and countless RPG games released over the last few decades. They do, however, maintain a couple of the similarities to the elves we are used to seeing. They have much longer lifespans than us humans, an ancient and magical history, a penchant for xenophobia, and forms of naturalistic magic.

I've built many details throughout the series to give these elves a unique place, even though they are a relatively minor part of my story. For one, a major historical event that drives the relations between the antagonist and the elves and figures deeply into the last book was included, and it really links the larger world together while providing ample backstory for my main baddie.

The elves also have a long history, and we are meant to feel that throughout the story, even if we don't get to see much of it. I also use the lore of a great elven city that few humans have ever seen. Elven males get tattoos on their faces full of ancient elven script, which can be a bit exotic for humans and other races to see for the first time. They are scrappy horsemen with tatted-up faces and a severe prejudice against humans.

Did I make them unique enough to justify the use of an overused race like elves?

Only the readers can answer that question, but I did try my best.

The main theme of these one-dimensional races is something often called *not-quite human*. It's when a writer creates a race that's human except for a few minor differences. Some examples are merfolk (mermaids and their kin) who seem just like humans except they have a slightly different anatomy and are adapted to living underwater. The *beast-man* trope, which is essentially a large, hairy, often bellicose male, is another creature often encountered in fantasy and sci-fi. This trope has been so overdone in so-called "shifter romance" novels that it's become something of a parody.

Little cute people. A simple race smaller than humans, unthreatening and relatively harmless. Tolkien did a wonderful job using this type of character—namely hobbits—as hero characters who step out of the usual trope and out of their comfort zone to save the world.

Green-skinned space babes is another popular choice among writers. In sci-fi, it's common to have a beautiful race of women with the only noticeable difference from humans being green skin and wild eye/hair colors. Again, it's gotten to the point of parody where space comedy novels throw shade at this trope.

These examples show the shallow nature of lazy world-building. The idea should not be to create races who are *almost* human. The goal should be to create races who intrigue the reader and makes them think how they are different from humans and how those differences might lead to different behaviors, wants/desires, and ultimately to unique conflicts within the plot.

Yes, it's obvious that the wood elves don't want the humans to cut down the forest they've lived in since the dawn of time, but that storyline is too simple. We have endless variants of *Ferngully* and *Avatar* to explore that trope. These tropes often occur because the races are too shallow, and it becomes difficult for the writer to think of a conflict for the races beyond something they've seen countless times before in other stories.

Tom Pollock's *Skyscraper Throne* has some of the most unique and interesting creatures in all of fantasy. The sodiumites and blankleits are truly bizarre. They are essentially spirits that inhabit every streetlight in London. They hit their enemies with bursts of energy and intensify their power by coming together and engaging in a group dance.

What a way to make something as mundane as a streetlamp intriguing!

Writing **Tip:** Create races with unique angles or characteristics that aren't just filling in the not-quite-human mold and that complement your story. Better yet, create races that have built-in reasons for conflict with your protagonist/antagonist so you can gain elements of plot and character development from your world-building.

CHAPTER 6

Monolithic Social, Political, Cultural, and Religious Groups

This is a variation on the theme of our last chapter but worthy of a separate discussion. How many religious groups have you seen in fantasy and sci-fi that are just a shallow copy of the Catholic Church or Zen Buddhism? Probably more than you can count.

On the one hand, these stereotypical groups are reiterated again and again because they have had a profound influence on human thought and have many adherents around the world. On the other hand, they deal with a lot of the answers to the big questions people have always wondered about. It makes sense for writers to go back to the familiar, but it does get old.

TV Tropes—more on that reference later—refers to this as *Crystal Dragon Jesus*. A writer takes obvious attributes, some good and some bad, from Christianity and applies them to a fantasy religion. In Phillip Pullman's *His Dark Materials* series, we find the overdone anti-clerical, falsely puritanical sect acting in their own self-interests while pulling the wool over the eyes of the common people. In George R.R. Martin's *A Song of Ice and Fire* series, the Faith of the Seven returns to an extremist form of devotion after much of the Seven Kingdoms have been ravaged by warfare, leaving the "smallfolk" to question the nature of power afforded to the nobility.

Martin's dogmatic and zombie-like awakening of the Faith of the Seven is much more thought-provoking than the myriad stories of greedy, money-grubbing sects who come across as flat and derivative of the obvious issues we face with organized religions in our daily lives here on Earth. We *know* the High Septon is a disturbed and dangerous man, but he also responds effectively to the sentiment of the people and gives them an avenue to make their voices heard. At one point, he even manages to imprison Queen Cersei, torturing and humiliating her in front of the entire populace of King's Landing. Talk about a power play and role-reversal packed into one punch. They engaged in economic and religious populism before it was cool to do so.

Writing Tip: If you must be derivative, then give the derivation a unique angle. I am repulsed by the actions of the Faith of the Seven, but I enjoy watching them make the nobles' experience a hint of the misery they have created for the local populace of King's Landing and the rest of the Seven Kingdoms through endless warfare and taxation.

In C.S. Lewis's *The Chronicles of Narnia*, Aslan is Jesus in all but name and form. I'm not criticizing this. In fact, I find it amazing that Lewis is able to make such a memorable character from something so transparent. And who could forget the *Dragonlance* series with their Church of Paladine and the Holy Triad? One of my favorites comes from *Stranger in a Strange Land* by Robert A. Heinlein. The character, Valentine Michael Smith, starts a cult centered around peace and loving others, which sounds familiar to those of us who attended Sunday School. He is brutally murdered, just like another famous religious revolutionary you might be familiar with, before ascending into a higher state of existence. These bits and pieces are taken from real-world religion, but it's so well executed and built that it reads as brilliant world-building and top-notch literary theme.

What about more original takes on religion? In Roger Zelazny's *Lord of Light*, we are given a new take with a sort of east meets west approach to sci-fi. In a far-off future, settlers from Earth want to colonize a planet full of alien life forms, seeking to use the advanced technologies available to them to project god-like abilities and appearances with a strong Hindi/Buddhist vibe. Things quickly get intense! It's one of the most interesting takes on Earth religion derivations in sci-fi I've ever come across, and a must-read for any sci-fi and fantasy writer.

Many fantasy stories in the West are derivative of the political and social structures of Medieval Europe, more specifically England, but if you hop across the Pacific, you'll find countless stories based on historical China, with fantasy elements like mythical creatures and magic, and everyone with impossibly white skin. It's not wrong to give your world the superstructure of an ancient society, in fact, it provides a nice line from which you can make changes!

A writer can start asking themselves important what-if questions like, what if the Christ figure hadn't been murdered? What would have happened? Could I make an interesting social, religious, and political narrative with this drastic departure? I think the answer is a most-assured yes.

What about a society with roots in the traditions of the Arctic Inuit? Of course, there are stories set in extreme cold environments, but perhaps there is some interesting daylight left to be written about these little-known people. What about a world set in the future where the governments have sprung from the massive, industrialized cities of New York, Los Angeles, Chicago, Dallas, and others? Where the U.S. territories are now controlled by cities backed by powerful, super rich corporate overlords? Take a simple what-if question, water it, and let it grow.

In terms of political entities, the vast majority of fantasy and sci-fi worlds operate either under kingdoms, dictatorships, or global democracies. A famous example would be The Galactic Republic of the *Star Wars Universe*, a federal parliamentary republic comprised of thousands of separate worlds. It's wildly ambitious for such a system, spanning such incredible distances and species to hold together for as long as it did, but such systems are relatively common in the genre, as surprising as that may be.

If you would like to create a democracy, one of the first things to consider is the question of voting rights. Who can vote? It's certainly not a given that your society agrees with the concept of universal suffrage. Perhaps only university graduates have the right to vote, or heads of households, or only women, or even only children? Orson Scott Card found an interesting way to incorporate children into the most important levels of the military in *Ender's Game*. A writer might be able to incorporate children into other domains where we would normally be dismissive of them.

Do you want the theme of the political structure to give a positive or negative feeling to the protagonist? Do you want a mix of feelings? The answers to these questions will help your democracy come to light as you build your world. You might very well be able to pull off a total democracy where every citizen votes and has an equal say, but there are lots of interesting alternatives for you to explore. How strong or weak is the state's power? Are they firmly in control or is their power threatened? What are the main parties and cliques inside the political structure?

❄

How educated are the citizens? Do they know politics and important policy issues well or are they led by propaganda? How long do representatives serve and what is their power?

How will you lay out the social structure? Specifically, the unwritten rules about how older people interact with younger people, the different genders, and how they perceive each other, rich to poor, educated to uneducated, and so many more. Pick a couple aspects of culture that interest you and put your own creative spin on them.

In Jim Henson's *The Dark Crystal* and follow-up Netflix television series *The Dark Crystal: Age of Resistance*, the main characters are mostly gelflings. This magical species has a matriarchy. The female gelflings rule over regions while a high matriarch oversees those regions. The female gelflings also have wings and can fly, unlike the males. Imagine the social implications of a female-led society where the females could fly wherever they wanted to go. It's great high concept and thought-provoking. I loved it.

Equally fun could be creating a dictatorship, not to be confused with a traditional monarchy with a royal family and such. A dictatorship usually revolves around the strong will of a male leader. You could flip this on its head in many ways. Obviously, you could make a strong female or non-binary dictator, or you could put a weakling in the dictator's position. Why a weakling? Because it's interesting to subvert the standard. Readers will be thinking: "How is the writer going to make this believable? I better keep reading to see how this turns out." As the creative artist, you *will* make your weakling dictator work. If he doesn't work, you will have an interesting plot to work through along the way.

Before we put a period on this topic, I would suggest you try taking a world that *seems* monolithic or seems a lot like our societies here on Earth and focus on a particularly counter-cultural group or element. Keep drilling down until you flesh it out in a unique way, and readers will talk about your original and thematic world-building for years to come.

O r so we all dream. =)

※

W riting Tip: Strive to awe the reader with amazing new takes on old topics or give them an element of culture rarely touched upon. This will differentiate you from the crowded field of writers while creating a memorable experience for the reader.

CHAPTER 7

No Sense of Place

I n online writer's groups, other authors and I have shared chapters of our fledgling stories or entire short stories between the group in order to get feedback and try to identify potential problems in our writing. The process was quite useful, and I felt myself "level up" quickly as I took the advice of more experienced writers to heart.

One thing I often noticed in the works I was reading and critiquing were fantasy and sci-fi stories that took location almost completely for granted. Perhaps it was that the writer was planning to pepper more elements conveying location throughout later chapters, but from what I had read, that was rarely the case.

A story about a race of aliens—humanoid but also squid-like—lived on a water planet with strange structures that the readers were just left to imagine completely for themselves. It always felt so shallow just to be given a generic water world—or other such location—as the entire focus of the story. Often, they seemed hastily created to cover for an on-the-nose love triangle plot.

What's the point of coming up with interesting aliens just to make them live and act like humans on Earth and for their world to be just a water Earth? It was so hard to get into those stories.

I've read many urban fantasies that revolve around teen protagonists who would either come into contact with a secret society of vampire or dragon shifters—or the teen was one of those creatures trying to fit in to modern society. When we'd visit the world of these fantasy creatures, I was interested to see what kind of amazing world-building the writer had created for us readers, only to be disappointed because there were no unique elements. Just a shallow attempt to push a story about not fitting into modern life. It's such a missed opportunity to not give the secret society some angle of appeal or to perhaps provide a criticism of their strange ways.

Location is a key aspect of theme.

If you nurture and grow it, your location can tell a story by itself. Diana Young's *Ferngully*, Disney's *Pocahontas*, and James Cameron's *Avatar*—though all highly derivative of books like *The Last of the Mohicans*—all developed their story in different ways through the location and environment. *Ferngully* and *Avatar* have obvious plot derivations. Even though they are both tackling destruction of sacred forests, the world-building aspects of those forest locations are wildly different. Take a look at the creatures that live on Pandora, a fictional moon of the planet Polyphemus. The atmosphere is unbearable for humans, who need to wear oxygen masks on the surface of Pandora, giving the location a very harsh feel, but the amazing Na'vi people roam the land with a powerful roar. The mineral unobtainium creates a type of superconductivity within the geology of the moon, leading to amazing floating mountains and a bio-connection among the plants and animals that live there.

This location is alive despite us having read this type of story so many times before. And the box-office records *Avatar* broke shows that even derivative stories can have amazing success if the world and characters are interesting enough.

In Michael End's novel, *The Neverending Story*, which most of us came to know through its film adaptation, we are taken to the world of Fantastica—Fantasia in the movie—a place where fairy tales are as real as the children who believe in them. One of the most iconic locations is the Ivory Tower.

In the novel, the Ivory Tower isn't actually a tower. It's a huge city built-up like a modern skyscraper with the Childlike Empress ruling from high atop.

In both the novel and the film adaptation, the Ivory Tower isn't described in detail, yet a feeling of wonder and awe is conveyed. It is memorable to anyone who has read this story or seen the movie. It wasn't a terribly difficult part of the story for the author to implement, since it's essentially a shiny white tower where the magic happens.

Another favorite of mine from sci-fi is the *Heritage Universe* created by Charles Sheffield. The primary feature of this location(s) is a set of huge ancient artifacts created by a long-gone race known only as The Builders.

One example of these artifact locations is called The Cocoon. The Cocoon appears to have been created out of one of the moons of the planet Savalle, as history accounts for two moons but only one remains. This artifact allows for a large amount of material to be transferred from the planet below to other locations at a highly accelerated rate. All the artifact locations in this series are highly mysterious and have different purposes, but they are one of the key aspects of location and world-building that makes *The Foundation* series so memorable.

W **riting Tip:** Define your location well enough so readers will be drawn in and intrigued, instead of using location as four semi-invisible walls where your characters hang out.

A final note on location, and perhaps the one that can give your location the biggest boost of all. Incorporate smells and sights into your locations. Tell us about the bread the protagonist smells baking as he walks past the bakery. Describe the sound of children laughing as they run down the alley playing with their toys, describe the sour taste of an undercooked dish that a character has to pretend they like so as not to offend their hosts.

Here is an excerpt from *Daughter of Dragons*, the final book in my *Daughter of Havenglade* series, which displays what I think is a normal level of world-building of the five senses variety.

"They walked down a wide alley packed with folks looking for bargains and vendors selling their wares. A butcher chopped the hindquarters of a pig on a large wooden block while a short, bespectacled woman with her hair tied back in a ponytail hollered out prices for pig's feet, intestines, shoulders, and tail. Laurena especially liked pig's tail fried in oil with pepper and onions. The thought alone made her stomach growl."

It would have been easy for me to avoid writing about the protagonist merely walking from her aunt's home to the *Torba Inn & Tavern*, but those few sentences established some aspects of daily life on the streets of the city. There are examples of this peppered throughout, as the characters travel to different locations. I didn't want to fall into the *four-empty-walls* habit where every location is generic and forgettable.

How can you make a city interesting and unique without spending loads of time planning it?

Writers can use a method similar to the geography examples I've provided. Create something unusually linear or focus on a particularly odd feature of the city or village.

For example, what if there was a city made of gold somewhere in your world? On Earth, gold is a valuable and relatively rare resource, but there's no reason it should be that way on a secondary world. Amazingly, the locals shrug when foreign traders remark on all the buildings constructed with gold. The only reason these gold-flooded locals need concern themselves with the value of gold is when they need to stop foreign bandits from breaking off chunks of their shops and hovels in the dark of night with dreams of returning to their homelands rich beyond their wildest dreams.

Plenty of conflicts generate almost like magic from this method of world-building. How about a domed city on the Martian surface? The first of its kind, run by a corporation with little to no government/public oversight. What conflicts naturally spring forth from this kind of world? Will the employees and volunteers living on a world far from the protective powers of police, media coverage, and societal dictates still have the same problems as people living on a city back on Earth? Or will these unique circumstances lead to new conflicts, new habits, and new cultural practices?

Of course, that is for you, the writer, to decide. There are certainly opportunities for interesting conflict inherent in this type of world-building

Did you instead want to focus on the peculiar? What if characters started hearing voices from down inside the village well after they gathered water each day? Or what if a zoo with magical animals, such as dragons, manticores, and all manner of fantastic beasts, was founded in the protagonist's city? What could go wrong? Remember *Jurassic Park*?

In Stephen King's fantasy novel, *The Eyes of the Dragon*, there is an immense tower in the city center known as The Needle. The Needle is central to the plot of the story as the protagonist is forced to spend a great deal of time there. It's no more than an unusually tall tower, but it helps bring the location of the story to life as readers can center themselves on the tower in a way not unlike the city is centered around the tower. It's a point of reference that gives structure to the rest of the city.

In *The Wonderful Wizard of Oz*, L. Frank Baum takes us to the Emerald City, which we could look at as a type of variation on my city of gold idea from earlier in the chapter. There isn't much explanation for why the city needed to be made of emeralds, but it was an obvious way to make the city unique, grandiose, and fantastical. Which do you think is more memorable to readers? The Yellow Brick Road or the Emerald City?

It's a tough question to answer.

The Gatsby Mansion in F. Scott Fitzgerald's literary masterpiece *The Great Gatsby* is not from a fantasy or sci-fi novel, but it's an iconic piece of world-building. To me, it is so much more than just a huge, decadent house for a wealthy bachelor. The character of Jay Gatsby makes it so much more, but I would argue if readers went back to look over the scenes that take place in the Gatsby Mansion, they'll find these scenes flow smoothly without any intimate detail. Fitzgerald wasn't focused on the house, he was focused on the story. Incredibly, he created a very memorable piece of world-building that might have felt otherwise unnecessary at the time of his writing.

In my *Daughter of Havenglade* series, a simple location that occurs in all four books is a set of cabins in the Dorbon Forest. These cabins are the home of Wizard Unai, my protagonist Laurena Blackwood's teacher. I don't go into much detail of the cabins as structures, but a lot of important scenes in character and plot development take place in and around those cabins. The characters make the cabins memorable and familiar to the reader because they fill the nondescript place with life. That's a case wherein the lack of detail in world-building allowed for a location to be what it needed to be, which paradoxically is sometimes the blank four walls that descriptive writing teachers rail against.

Writing Tip: Consider letting important plot reveals and moments of powerful character interaction take place in less-developed locations. Save your well-developed locations for lighter scenes, so the descriptive world-building can help carry the load and fill in without feeling like it's slowing down the story.

CHAPTER 8

Where Does the Magic Come From?

If your world has a magic system or even the presence of magic, it's vital that the reader gets a sense of what is possible and what isn't within that magic system. The boundaries of your magic system help to add a sense of depth and realism to an otherwise unrealistic situation.

For example, if the reader has the impression that the hero can use their magic to get out of any possible trouble or to defeat every possible villain, you lose all sense of stakes.

"Hey! The stakes are supposed to be a matter of plot. How can world-building effect the stakes?"

Simple.

Think about *Superman*. The writers have to keep finding new ways to get Superman near kryptonite—a super rare element from outside of the solar system. This tiny Achilles' heel means that Superman almost never seems like he's in any danger no matter what kind of ridiculous situation he's thrown into.

They often have to put people close to Superman at risk to create any sense of stakes in the plot. Think of how many times Lois

Lane has been kidnapped, taken hostage, or used against Superman in one way or another. That's not to say Superman isn't a character that many people love, it's just much harder to establish stakes with an overpowered character compared to a hero with vulnerabilities.

Compare Superman's vulnerabilities to Batman's vulnerabilities. Yes, Batman is mega-rich, smart, good-looking, and knows how to kick ass with all kinds of high-tech devices, but in the end, he is not *super*. He's made up of the same stuff as you and me. If you prick his finger, he bleeds; if you shoot him, he might die. He's also very messed-up psychologically, leading to his own defeat sometimes. In many ways, Batman's most formidable adversary is himself.

That wasn't about magic systems, but I think the point is related. Prolific fantasy writer Brandon Sanderson has something he calls *Sanderson's Second Law*, which essentially expresses to writers that it isn't what heroes *can* do that is most important to who they are, but what they have trouble doing—or can't do at all—that make them interesting.

Perhaps in your story, when wizards apply their power, they age. That would mean the wizards would have to be careful about when and where they use it. A limitation of this sort is reminiscent of the comic book *Spawn* by Todd McFarlane. Spawn is a superhero who bought his way out of hell, but at a price. A deal with the devil. He's given amazing powers from the underworld but when these powers run out, he's got a one-way ticket back to hell, so he'd better make each use of power count. The series features an illustrated timer that shows how much power he has left after using his magic.

In my *Daughter of Havenglade* series, there are a couple of different magical systems. The most important one is a form of magic practiced by a select few who are chosen for their unique gifts to bond with a powerful crystal. The drawbacks include the crystal needing time to bond for each use and can't be used on a split-second notice. Some characters refer to this as *warming.* The crystal also only allows a certain amount of energy to be used within a short time. More powerful and experienced wizards and enchantresses are able to squeeze more magic from their crystals. How that translates is through the protagonist Laurena Blackwood becoming worn out quickly and sometimes can't rely on her magic to get her out of trouble.

Perhaps in your story, the use of magic presents a drain on the world around the wizards? In *The Dark Crystal: Age of Resistance,* a dangerous energy called the Darkening—which is also known as the Blight—flows from the Crystal of Truth whenever it is damaged. It appears as a purple or black vapor and kills the plants around it. If an animal consumed it, they would become aggressive and eventually be killed by this form of magic. Emperor skekSo's body is revealed to be falling apart in an episode of *The Dark Crystal: Age of Resistance* because of his experimenting and harnessing of the power of the Darkening.

This particular drawback is interesting when combined with evil characters who seek power at all costs. Thematically, knowing how magic works in this instance and the risks from using it, we are able to learn more about the characters based on how they react to the dangerous power.

Writing Tip: Use drawbacks and weaknesses more than strengths and powers when designing and describing your magic system. It's easy to make overpowered superheroes. It's difficult to make heroes who need to make tough decisions because life presents them with dilemmas their magic can't get them out of.

CHAPTER 9

A One Stop Shop to Up Your World-Building Game

As I mentioned at the outset, this section of the book is for writers who don't want to world-build much or are merely toying with the idea. Many writers are looking for a hack, a world-building *CliffsNotes*, or for it to be laid out in front of them to easily digest. Well, they are in luck. There is a great website available that can fill you in on all the popular aspects of both fantasy and sci-fi world-building and elements of story that we see repeated and should be familiar with.

It's called *TV Tropes*.

This website offers examples of all the major and most of the minor tropes from literature, television, movies, and more. I know many successful indie authors who spend hours on end just reading through many of the wonderfully explained entries. It's easy to lose track of time when you're exploring down different rabbit holes on *TV Tropes*.

For our examples, let's focus on *TV Tropes* Sci-fi and *TV Tropes* Space, two subcategories full of valuable information for world-building—and plot/character development, too, but sadly that's outside the scope of this book.

In *TV Tropes* Sci-fi, it starts off by breaking down the most popular genres like space opera, steampunk, and cyberpunk. It's suggested that the defining feature that separates sci-fi from other genres is that there are some forms of technology that don't exist around the time period when the story was written. Think H.G. Wells's *The Time Machine*, which was published in 1895. We still don't have anything close to a machine that can allow people to travel through time.

The technology is the crucial aspect of world-building a writer will be challenged to get right in a sci-fi story. A writer can overcome many problems inherent in their writing if they can awe the reader with the technology. In Liu Ci Xin's Hugo winning novel, *The Three-Body Problem*, we get masterful and nuanced presentations of alien technology and out-of-the-box solutions on how to confront the threats these aliens present.

I read the entire series because the technology behind Ci Xin's world-building was so unique and interesting.

In cyberpunk, the world-building often revolves around a concept of "high-tech, low life". In other words, the characters have technological marvels, but their lives are as grimy and pointless as people living in the slums of our own societies of today. The protagonists often live in cramped and dirty apartment buildings on high floors of huge skyscrapers. They have voice-activated homes that open the door for them, turn on the lights, and make them coffee, but we are given the impression that all is not well. Progress has halted even as technology has improved.

In Ari Bach's *Valhalla,* everyone is connected to the internet. From childhood, a child's intellect is valued above all else. What better than to have a protagonist who is strong and gruff? This character has to deal with the fact that she was born in the wrong century, at a time where physical prowess is almost useless. As the plot progresses, the world-building flips things on its head, and suddenly she is exactly what the world needs. It's brilliant writing.

Do yourself a favor and read it.

In *TV Tropes* Space, stories revolve around massive spaceships, interstellar travel, and amazing space colonies. In these stories, the spaceship isn't just a highly important piece of world-building, it also acts as something of a character in the story. In the sci-fi horror film *Event Horizon,* the spaceship—of the same name—is equal parts haunted house and ghostly supervillain. The writers made sure to create a ship full of dark spaces and strangely shaped features. Scary noises abound in the spaceship, and it's not a place where you'd want to spend months on end, floating through the abyss of Outer Space.

Regardless of whether the spaceship is scary or not, it needs to stand out in sci-fi. If it's a military vessel, then the writer might focus on descriptions of weapons and defensive systems that will fascinate the reader. The spaceship might also have a weak spot. Perhaps its weapons take a longer to load, or it has some mechanical fault—something that makes the reader second-guess if all this amazing technology will be enough to save the day.

Portal networks are common technology in sci-fi. A popular example is from the *Stargate* franchise. It's in the title! The plot *depends on* the world-building of a literal portal network. Sure, the writers had to put an interesting culture and conflict on the other end of the portal—another piece of fantastic location-building, but the stargate allows the plot to spring forth like magic.

It gives the story a place to go—literally.

As you browse through *TV Tropes*, you will find some familiar themes and some you will fall in love with and want to incorporate into your stories. One popular trope in military sci-fi—especially on the cover art—is the trope called *unnecessarily large vessel*. The foreground of the cover art for many military sci-fi stories features a massive spaceship either in the heat of battle with smaller vessels swarming around it or heading toward a wildly colored planet or star system. This is a type of industry standard in world-building and helps readers identify the genre just by glancing at the thumbnail of the book cover while browsing on Amazon.

A final interesting example I will give you is the trope of *burial in space*. A writer can show off a bit of world-building that can greatly affect the theme, plot, and characterization by having a somewhat important character die during the journey and then using space technology to have a space funeral. A common but powerful plot device goes something like this—the captain has died, the second-in-command is not a good leader and has a natural conflict with the character around whom the crew rallies as the unspoken leader.

To wrap up my endorsement of *TV Tropes* as an amazing world-building resource, I encourage writers to browse the site—I have no relationship with it, though I wish I did!—it's truly a great place to catch up on the roots of world-building in your genre before deciding if you need to dig deeper.

W riting Tip: Explore the various resources available to you, whether that be at your local library, on the net, or from the mouths of other writers. There is more information available to us than at any other time and writers should put it to good use.

CHAPTER 10

To Pants or to Plot

Now, you might realize that a lot of what I've advocated and many of the examples of deep world-building I've presented are the result of careful planning. Many writers are discovery writers and are perfectly happy and competent to create great stories without a written plan in mind.

You can also discovery-write your world-building in a similar manner to how you write your story, though there will be more rewriting and backtracking if the elements don't mesh well together or if you realize you need to do more research after your writing session is over. World-building initially lends itself to plotters, but with a bit of practice, many writers have little trouble introducing interesting world-building details into their manuscripts.

You don't necessarily need to plot or outline world-building, though there is some upfront work you might consider investing a bit of time into, to see if it helps you pants your world-building even easier. In fantasy, one of the most beloved staples is a world map, or a map of the known world from the perspective of the protagonist's society. For those of you who cringe at the idea of trying your hand at visual arts, keep in mind that the map does not necessarily need to be presented to your readers in a full-color, high-definition image on a page. It can simply help your writing process.

It could be as simple as a few scribbles in a notebook of the basic placement of details, the names of the locations, if nothing else, to help the writer keep track of where cities are in relation to each other and approximately how far the locations referenced or visited in the story are from one another. This can be done in just a few moments, then referenced during the writing process when the writer is fuzzy on the details of how far the dark tower is from the hero's village, and roughly how many days it might take her to travel there by horseback or by griffin.

If you are on the other side and don't mind a bit of planning—or even enjoy it—you might consider checking out some of the easy-to-use fantasy mapping resources available. As someone with little to no visual-arts skills, I was greatly impressed with how easily I could produce a beautiful world map with the Inkarnate mapmaking website. I placed mountains, rivers, and coastlines in mere minutes. After a few days of coming back to it for a couple of minutes at a time when I had the free time, I had created a map I liked. This has really helped me with the lore and history of my upcoming fantasy series.

Again, I'm not connected to any of the resources I suggest in this book, but I will mention some websites like KBoards, YouTube, and many others that have helped me on my writing journey and that I think can help other writers looking to take the next step.

To plot your world-building, you may want to write down names for the last couple of leaders of your society, make a note or two about an important historical event that still affects the society to this day, and some of the more pertinent social ideas on the minds of the citizens and elites in your story. Keeping these things in mind allows a writer to easily move from their cozy writing desk on twenty-first-century Earth to a future Mars colony where ideas of progress and economy may vary wildly from how things are perceived back in our world.

Writing Tip: Whether you've decided on discovery writing or plotting, understand the ways in which you can make world-building easier for yourself and how to help it manifest itself creatively from your writing process.

CHAPTER 11

Real World or Secondary World

There are two worlds out there.

Well, there are actually an infinite number of worlds out there to create for a story. But the duality in fantasy worlds is the choice between so-called real world and secondary worlds. This choice will come about naturally as it's hard to start writing a story if you don't even know what world it takes place in.

In this chapter, I will provide a brief run-through of some of the more popular sub-genres and introduce a couple of authors and books in each genre that the reader can then research at their leisure.

Real-world stories are often broken up into fantasy sub-genres like urban fantasy, with some popular staples being Jim Butcher's *The Dresden Files*, Patricia Briggs's *Mercy Thompson* series, and Cassandra Clare's *The Mortal Instruments* series.

Urban fantasy tends to take place in or around the present day but adds otherwise supernatural elements to the world-building and plot. Remember, urban fantasy is not the same as paranormal romance—another hot sub-genre. Urban fantasy puts the fantasy first—the quest/missions are essential to the story. In paranormal romance, however, the romantic elements are essential, and thus the romance is put first.

Examples of paranormal romance include J.R. Ward's *Black Dagger Brotherhood* series, Stephenie Meyer's *Twilight* series, and Jeaniene Frost's *Night Huntress* series. In these fantasies, the romance is not just a random inclusion, but an essential aspect of plot and character development, which the readers expect. In fantasy stories, romance is optional—there are romantic fantasies, too—but the readers expect some sort of resolution of quest and development of ability.

Steampunk stories are usually classified as sci-fi because of the technologies inherent in their world-building. They tend to be real-world stories but based on an alternative history where ideas of nineteenth-century industrial steam-power is king. Popular locations for steampunk include Victorian England and the American Wild West. The Hollywood feature film, *Wild Wild West* starring Will Smith, is a well-known example of this trope.

The world-building in steampunk stories is heavily influenced by the perceived ideas of what people of the nineteenth century might have envisioned in regard to culture, art, fashion, language, etc. Some popular examples of steampunk sci-fi are Gail Carriger's *Parasol Protectorate* series, Scott Westerfeld's *Leviathan* series, and Cherie Priest's *Boneshaker*.

Cyberpunk is a sci-fi sub-genre written in a dystopian future which, as we mentioned previously, focuses on the trope of "high-tech, low life". Key thematic elements often include aspects borrowed from noir films and detective stories. Strong thematic representations of a troubled future and narratives that counter ideas of future utopias. The classic works in the genre include several works by Phillip K. Dick—including *Do Androids Dream of Electric Sheep?*, which I mentioned was the primary source material for the movie *Blade Runner* starring Harrison Ford—William Gibson's *Johnny Mnemonic* and *The Neuromancer*, as well as Neal Stephenson's *Snow Crash*.

A crossover between real-world and secondary-world fantasies is called portal fantasy. Think J.K. Rowling's *Harry Potter* series, C.S. Lewis's *The Chronicles of Narnia*, and Laini Taylor's *Daughter of Smoke and Bone* series. Portal fantasy include both our real world and a unique secondary world for readers to explore. Portal fantasies usually don't require much research on the real-world elements because most of the action takes place in the secondary world.

Fledgling fantasy and sci-fi writers may be wondering what constitutes a secondary world, and that's a great question that is essential to building your own unique world. My earliest understanding of secondary worlds came from Tolkien, who would describe them as consistent fantasy worlds that differed significantly from real-world fantasies.

Secondary world stories have many popular sub-genres, including epic fantasy with such well-known works as George R.R. Martin's *A Song of Ice and Fire*, Robert Jordan's *The Wheel of Time*, and Brandon Sanderson's *Mistborn*.

Epic fantasy—also referred to as high fantasy—is the genre readers think of when they want to follow a developing hero on a quest into the unknown or toward a final confrontation with a powerful villain. Epic can refer to either the noun, meaning a great story, or the adjective, which refers to the grand nature of the character, setting, themes, or plot inherent in these stories. Think good versus evil, and sword and sorcery, they often includes the dark lord trope.

Magical realism is a sub-genre containing the popular works like Neil Gaiman's *Stardust*, Erin Morgenstern's *The Night Circus*, and Patrick Rothfuss's *The Kingkiller Chronicles*. Magical realism can also take place in real-world stories like the incredible *One Hundred Years of Solitude* by Gabriel Garcia Marquez.

In magical realism, elements typical of fables and allegory are a major part of the plot, themes, and world-building. Magic is experienced in contrast to an otherwise mundane setting or location. Often, the fantasy elements blend natural and familiar themes with magic to express criticism on politics and culture.

Dark fantasy is a sub-genre that adds elements often associated with horror. The setting conveys a sense of dread or ominous outcomes to the reader. Popular titles in this sub-genre includes Anne Rice's *The Vampire Chronicles*, Neil Gaiman's *The Sandman*, and Stephen King's *The Dark Tower* series.

Writing Tip: Whether you are writing your sci-fi or fantasy story in the real world or a secondary world of your own creation, it's good to be familiar with the genre-defining books your readers are likely to have read. Your stories will inevitably be compared to the classics and popular works they share characteristics with. Careful research and world-building with an attention to detail will go a long way toward getting your story accepted the community of readers who love a particular genre.

CHAPTER 12

We Are ~~Not~~ Makers of History

Oh yes, we are!

As writers, we can create anything we put our minds to. As fantasy and sci-fi authors, it's our duty to flesh out details about the world we've created. Some of my favorite history and lore in fantasy world-building comes from George R.R. Martin's *A Song of Ice and Fire* series.

There were several key historical events that greatly influenced the plot of Martin's series. I'll talk about a few of them briefly. Hopefully, this can help get the creative juices flowing in your mind like they did for me when I was reading Martin's outstanding series.

Robert's Rebellion—also known by the losing Targaryens as the Usurping—was an uprising led by Robert Baratheon, who at the start of the story is the king of the Seven Kingdoms of Westeros. His allies were Jon Arryn, the Lord of the Eyrie, and Eddard Stark, the head of House Stark and Robert Baratheon's boyhood friend.

The primary trigger for Robert's Rebellion was the apparent kidnapping of Eddard Stark's sister Lyanna Stark by Prince

Rhaegar Targaryen. Lyanna was betrothed to Robert Baratheon at the time, and Rhaegar was already married with children.

Without delving too deeply into the details, Robert Baratheon struck down Prince Rhaegar at the Battle of the Trident, scoring a decisive victory for the rebellion, which led to the beginning of the story in *A Game of Thrones*.

That is just a brief description of a deeply plotted history, and one of the many events in the history of Westeros that influences the plot.

Martin digs deep into the history of many of his worlds, but you don't have to create a fully fleshed-out world like Westeros to provide the reader with a good sense of history and depth to your character's culture, which is always heavily influenced by history.

If you are writing military sci-fi, it's well worth the effort to create a bit of lore for your huge spaceship. A lot of the scenes will take place on the spaceship. Even when the characters disembark, they are still likely to reference their powerful transport.

Include a few lines early on that establish some of the history of the ship. Perhaps it was the only ship to survive a famous battle and was passed down to a young commander by a well-respected captain. The responsibility of taking care of the ship and the crew —and needing to do a better job than the previous captain did— now weighs heavily on the young captain.

Or perhaps it's the newest space cruiser right off the factory floor on its maiden voyage. The writer can reference what happened to the previous ship and create unexpected shortcomings for the hyped-up new ship that advance the plot and lead to interesting conflict.

Writers may also consider including a bit of family history to help establish the protagonist's or the antagonist's backstory. A common and successful trope is the orphan who just so happens to be the "chosen one". The kid has a rough childhood because the villain killed her parents and slowly grows in competency until the final showdown to avenge her past. Or the character had terrible parents and ran away from home at a young age, never to see his family again.

I n my fantasy murder mystery *The Inquisitor,* the protagonist Nestor Atias's family slowly fell apart as he grew up. His mother passed away, and his father continued to have troubles with local officials and powerful lords. Eventually, his father was forced out of his business and had to flee back to his homeland in shame, abandoning his adolescent son in a strange foreign land.

I keep the family history very brief with just a few sentences in the entire novel, but I think it's enough to give the character a backstory the readers need, so they can understand the strength of the protagonist better than they otherwise would have.

W riting Tip: Some well-placed details of a traumatic or character-building event from the character's past adds to your story's theme, giving your world a more-than-meets-the-eye moment when the events come full circle. Your story can become a tragedy when characters fail to grow from the events from their history. Or they can achieve real growth by overcoming the barriers placed in front of them by the ghosts of their haunted past.

I t's also worth taking note of Martin's world-building of the Summer Isles. We never visit the Summer Isles—as least we haven't so far in the main series (and I'm still waiting on *The Winds of Winter* but not holding my breath) but the bits of information we are given about this mysterious place is mainly derived from Martin's research on traditional African culture and traditions.

He makes it sound like a fascinating place that rival the culture in Westeros. He does introduce us to several important minor characters from the Summer Isles. Xara Xhoan Daxos is the rich patron in the fabled city of Qarth, who—if we believe the story he told Daenerys Targaryen—worked his way up from being an impoverished boy on the docks to the richest man in the most opulent city in the known world. Salladhor Saan is something of a charismatic pirate-smuggler, who lends his fleet to Stannis Baratheon in the hopes of great riches once Stannis claims the Iron Throne, and of course, Grey Worm. Grey Worm is the undisputed leader of the Unsullied, a deadly fighter, a loyal subject, and in the TV series, he is the beloved of Daenerys Targaryen's trusted advisor/handmaiden Missandei—a clever girl who knows many languages and also hails from a small island in the Summer Sea.

We are told that the people of Missandei's homeland are peaceful. There are no bastards on her home island of Naath because the concept of marriage, at least as far as the people of Westeros know it, doesn't exist.

People in Westeros and Essos both make claims that sex-positive prostitution exists in the Summer Isles. These women are respected and not looked down upon by society. Such minor world-building details have the power to make readers consider issues and positions they may never have considered before.

As a reader, it was intriguing to learn more about the mysterious places at the edges of the *A Song of Ice and Fire* world map. The culture and history of the Summer Isles are developed enough to feel real and intriguing, even though they play a minor role in the main plot of the epic.

For anyone writing military sci-fi or space opera, it's par for the course to provide a bit of history early on to set the stage for the futuristic world. This doesn't need to consist of a long dense prologue but can, in fact, be brief comments on the state of affairs and how far in the future the story takes place.

In *Dune*, Frank Herbert doesn't go into deep detail—at least not at the start of the first book—on the history of the vast galactic empire. We get a few clues early on without any long information dumps—thank heavens. We start to learn about the history and culture of the world by following a powerful family known as House Atreides, and then we follow the young protagonist Paul

Atreides as he navigates through the dangerous game of political intrigue and planetary management.

Writing Tip: Give readers interesting characters they can invest into early on. Provide references to the character's history and culture without forcing the reader to read through information dumps, and you will keep many readers eagerly wondering what comes next.

How do I know when I can present world-building up front in a way that is intriguing to readers?

That's an important question we should ask ourselves whenever we start providing explanations for our worlds. A good example comes from the prologue in *The Eye of the World* by Robert Jordan in his legendary *The Wheel of Time* series. The readers are given a look at the history with references to the Hundred Companions, who were a group of young men from the Age of Legends. Jordan gives the reader details on the Dark One, the force of evil throughout the series, and we are given a scene of the aftermath of a truly violent and disturbing event. The character, Lewis Therin Telamon, finds his palace destroyed, corpses littering the grounds, and is in an absolute mental wreck himself.

The genius of this prologue, in my opinion, is that Jordan packs bite-sized bits of world-building into the narrative with characterization and an eerie and mysterious point of view scene. No information dumps. No long lists of royal dynasties.

It's a brilliantly written prologue. I've learned a lot from analyzing it.

CHAPTER 13

On Constructed Languages

Since you're reading into the deeper sections of this world-building guide, I won't pull any punches. Let's start with the more hardcore aspects of world-building.

Constructed languages have become such a mainstay of sci-fi and fantasy novels and movies these days. You may forget how fringe they were not so long ago. I can still remember the concept of Klingon in the *Star Trek Universe* being a meme before memes were even a thing.

Want to present someone as a nerd or otherwise socially inept individual back in the '90s? Tell everyone they learned how to speak Klingon. Even fans who loved *Star Trek* treated Klingon like a bridge too far. When Marc Okrand released the extended version of *The Klingon Dictionary* people went bananas. The book included pronunciation, vocabulary, and grammar and was originally intended to help the writers and actors. It built a modest cult following, which led to it being sold as a fan-targeted product.

Why was *The Klingon Dictionary* so noteworthy at the time?

I have my own ideas on that. I think for many who were intrigued with the space opera elements of popular movies like *Star Wars* and were more mild Trekkies, it just felt like a depth that they didn't expect from sci-fi, especially one based on a television show.

Tolkien had already created his elvish languages half a century before, and those languages were much more developed than Klingon, so did fantasy have a level of leeway afforded to it that popular sci-fi still hadn't reached? It's certainly possible.

In recent years, there have been several conlangs (constructed languages) featured prominently in blockbuster television and movie successes like High Valyrian and Dothraki in the *Game of Thrones* television series, and Na'vi from James Cameron's *Avatar*. Let's take a look at some of these examples to figure out if constructed languages could enhance your world-building and why it might be just what you are looking for.

Language creator David J. Peterson was brought on to bring the languages of Dothraki and High Valyrian to life in *A Game of Thrones*. He was given broad leeway, with the only guidelines being to use the words and phrases already printed in Martin's novels, of which only a few existed at the time of the television production.

Dothraki is the language of a nomadic war-faring people. These horse masters have always reminded me a bit of what I'd imagine the Mongols of old to have been like. The language Peterson produced sounds harsh, but the influences of Arabic and Spanish make it quite interesting to listen to, even though I have no idea what is being said without the help of the subtitles.

High Valyrian is a language of literature and a somewhat dead language in the *Song of Ice and Fire* world that occupies a similar place as Classical Chinese or Latin does. These types of languages were used to write many ancient and important documents, as well as works of poetry and literature, but the spoken versions mutated into different modern dialects, relegating the parent language to a status of scholarly and prestigious use.

Interestingly, High Valyrian even had a free study program active on the language learning application *Duolingo* at the time of this writing.

In the Nine Free Cities of Essos, differing forms of Bastard Valyrian are spoken. For example, Astapori Valyrian, Meereenese Valyrian, and the Slaver's Bay dialects. The languages of Dothraki and Valyrian were well-received by many fans of the A *Game of Thrones* franchise. YouTube is chock-full of videos of fans reciting lines from the TV show in these constructed languages.

One of the most iconic scenes from A *Game of Thrones* features Daenerys Targaryen seemingly trading one of her young dragons to a rich and vulgar slave-lord for an army of well-trained slaves. With the help of subtitles, the viewers understood that the trader had been making rude remarks about Daenerys throughout the negotiations in Astapori Valayrian, but the trader's translator conveyed the messages to Daenerys with more tact. From our point of view, she seemed to not know about his uncouth insults, but the moment the army becomes hers, she starts commanding them in High Valyrian, shocking those around her.

She gives a fiery response to the trader when he complains with curses that the young dragon won't obey him. I will paraphrase, but she essentially says dragons are not slaves and uses the local word for slave to emphasize that she understood the vulgarities he had been spouting. In a powerful moment for her character, she tells them her name and that she is not just some nobody, that there is greatness in her bloodline, and that Valyrian is her mother language. She then commands the little dragon to burn the slave-trader alive.

I suggest watching this masterful scene to see how much power a constructed language can add to characterization.

For Cameron's sci-fi blockbuster film *Avatar*, Professor Paul Frommer was tasked with creating a language for the alien beings who lived on a distant moon called Pandora. One of Cameron's goals was for the language to sound unlike any one human language, and this resulted in Na'vi. Na'vi has since gained a strong following through the Lexical Expansion Project, which seeks to expand the depth of the language and introduce people to Na'vi.

Why did the practice of adding fully formed constructed languages to works of sci-fi and fantasy catch on in such a way?

Remember, the languages I've mentioned are fully formed, meaning they have a complete grammar set, a phonetic inventory, morphology, pronunciation, and extensive lexicons. It's not just babble.

I think readers have become used to deeper aspects of world-building and even casual fans are now appreciating the chance to delve into the story and the elements built around it. It also shows the readers and viewers that the creators are putting a lot of effort into their creations. They aren't shallow shells put together just to make money. There is artistic care taken to ensure the stories are unique and interesting.

All right, that's a basic look at a few conlangs in popular culture. For writers who have decided to put some form of constructed language into their stories, I suggest considering whether you need a fully developed language or just a naming language.

A naming language is primarily used for filling out names of geographical locations and cities on a map and to provide interesting names for characters in your story. It won't require much more than a wordlist and a basic outline.

I've included several references to Tolkien's fully developed Elvish, but did you know Tolkien also employed naming languages? Tolkien's Black Speech was made famous because it is the language used on the beautiful inscription of The One Ring, which is essentially the only time readers and viewers get a chance to experience this naming language.

To get started, I recommend listing the sounds you would like to use or at least note the ones you want to include that aren't found in English. Don't make this list too long, as this won't help much if you are just creating names.

You can play around with different sound patterns like /tat/, /zyn/, /ugi/ or whatever patterns you find appealing.

I've found it easiest to start with names for rivers, mountains, oceans, and lakes. Geographical names are a good place to start because you can create some useful adjectives that greatly increases the lexicon without adding much time to the creation. Think of it like this, if your language has ten useful nouns, then every time you create one adjective, you are adding at least ten possible new names in your language. Create adjectives for words like long, old, tall, short, big, small, green, blue, terrible, beautiful, etc. and then you can add these to the geography terms to create words like "big mountain", "long river", and so on.

Use repeated elements across your map. It doesn't make sense for every place and feature to have a truly unique name. If you study "real world" maps, you will see the same words repeated in many places.

Writing Tip: Remember, at its heart, world-building is an attempt to create a sense of reality for the reader to sink into, not to bog them down with an overload of uniqueness. The beauty and art of world-building lies in *blending* unique elements with the more mundane. Removing all the mundane or adding too much quirkiness is like cooking with too much salt or sugar. Both can enhance taste when added in moderation, but if you pour in the whole bag, you'll have a mess that no one wants to eat.

The sound inventory I mentioned can be divided up into consonants and vowels in your notebook or Excel spreadsheet. For those interested in taking up the hobby to learn more about linguistics in general, you can start separating them into a true phonetic inventory with classes like labial, dental, velar, and other categories based on place of articulation, etc.

Don't just include all the sounds in English and the ones you've added. This just creates an "English Plus" language. Make sure you remove certain sounds as well to give it a more unique sound identity.

Keep all your words in an alphabetically listed lexicon/dictionary. This way you can find the word you need quickly so as not to waste too much time. Or worse yet, use the wrong word because you can't find the one you wanted to use.

Naming languages aren't too much work to create and can be rewarding, since readers will feel like you've done something clever— if you have taken the time to make sure it sounds and reads consistent.

Most writers won't need to produce fully formed constructed languages for their story, but you may want to.

I'm working on several constructed languages for my next epic fantasy series. I've started with a semi-dead language from which to derive some modern languages. The first one is called Old Lunarian. It operates in a way not unlike a High Valyrian or Classic Chinese. In my next fantasy world, many texts are preserved in this language. Modern Lunarian's two dialects will be derived from Old Lunarian. I will include some interesting dialogue and story elements that highlight the languages in my stories to make my language more than just a way to show foreign culture. It will be a part of the characterization, plot, and theme.

For me, it's not just about the writing. I find conlanging to be a worthy and challenging hobby, and it has taught me a lot about languages. I'm only a fluent speaker in American English and Mandarin Chinese, both of which are SVO languages. That is, the basic sentence structure is subject + verb + object. For example, in English "I eat pizza." and in Mandarin Chinese 我吃比萨。Finally, with Pinyin pronunciation and tone markers it's: "wǒ chī bǐ sà." I decided to make Old Lunarian a VSO language, which has a basic structure of verb + subject + object. Instead of the word order, "The teacher reads the book" we would have, "Reads the teacher the book". Many language families use this structure, including Afroasiatic languages like Egyptian, Assyrian, Arabic, and Biblical Hebrew, as well as such distinct language families as Celtic— think Irish, Welsh, and Cornish; Mayan languages, Austronesian languages like Tagalog, Tongan, Maori, and Hawaiian, plus some Meso-American languages.

I added noun cases to Old Lunarian's grammar—also known as declensions. Contemporary English does very little with noun cases outside of pronoun usage, i.e. how we use he/him to distinguish subject from object. Chinese grammar does almost nothing with inflection, though there are several particles that express aspect and sometimes grammatical mood.

Needless to say, I was going to have a hard time working on a VSO language with noun declensions based on my own language background. So, I started studying Latin. Latin has tons of declensions, and though Latin word order is quite flexible, the SOV word order would help me get out of my element so I could start to accept unfamiliar grammatical patterns.

Writing Tip: Below are the basic steps I recommend for creating your own developed conlang as painlessly as possible.

1) <u>Create a phonetic inventory</u> – This is merely a list of the sounds that are present in your conlang.

2) <u>Develop phonetic constraints</u> – These are the rules dictating the possible phoneme sequences in a language. For example, the sounds e, t, and n in English. If you are a native speaker, you can arrange these three letters in their six possible combinations and know which are illegal constructions. Net, ent, and ten are legal. Nte, etn, and tne are illegal constructions. Words like tne are impossible because plosive + nasal clusters do not occur at the beginning of any word in the English language.

3) <u>Start creating words</u> – Combine sounds from your phonetic inventory that follow the rules of your phonetic constraints. The largest portion of your time spent on conlanging will most likely be spent here, as vocabulary is the limiting factor on what

can be produced in a language. You might end up feeling satisfied at around five hundred words, if they are focused on what needs to be said in your story and used on your world map. Others might be happier once their language hits the thousand-word mark as they will be able to express quite a bit more without constantly adding new words and expanding grammatical forms.

4) Select a grammar set – Decide which grammar forms will be necessary for you to express the information you want in your story. The use of tenses and which ones. Noun phrase word order; verb phrase word order; sentence structure VSO, SVO, OSV, or something else; how to ask questions; personal pronouns; singular/plural nouns; and whatever else you find necessary to express yourself through your new language.

5) Work on translation – Write down some basic translations to make sure you've included all the elements you need and aren't making grammatical mistakes. Basic sentences like "I like dragons", "Where is that scary cave?", "Yes, I can ride a horse", and other such structures will be useful once you need to translate a sentence for your story.

If you follow these steps, you should have little trouble achieving your goal of a usable and consistent constructed language that readers will be in awe of. There are many resources for learning more about constructed languages online. I've included many useful links in the back of this book. The linguistic articles on the Wikipedia are also extremely useful, in-depth sources one can use to find interesting language elements. I sometimes search random languages to see what kind of elements are present.

For more on-demand answers, you can join one of the many conlang groups networking through various social media platforms.

❄

CHAPTER 14

More on Real World Versus Secondary World...and Shifters

If a writer chooses to set a sci-fi or fantasy story in the real world, they still need to come up with world-building elements, though much less than they would have if they'd chosen a secondary world. One of the difficulties in writing in the real world is to make sure the research done on factual locations or on factual events and people have no continuity errors.

I'll never forget putting down a book for good after the third instance of the writer suggesting Brazilians mostly spoke Spanish —never mentioning Portuguese—apparently assuming this based on Brazil's location in Latin America. Don't make those kinds of embarrassing mistakes. Hopefully, we have thoughtful and talented editors to help us fix any glaring mistakes before our books reach the shelves.

For sci-fi, the elements writers add to the real world are mostly a matter of revealing how society and technology are different. The elements of theme, characterization, and plot will show readers how the story deals with those elements in your world. For fantasy works, writers get to define the magical system, mythical creatures, and societal norms and situations, which may vary greatly from our own.

I n the *Blade* franchise, Wesley Snipes plays the part of a dhampir, which as far as I can tell, is a human with a vampire's strengths but with few if any of their traditional weaknesses. He protects us normal folk from vampires. The story reveals a secret battle between vampires and dhampirs. The world-building sets the stage for the plot and the tension within the story.

W **riting Tip:** The best world-building is the type that blends with other elements of story such as concept, story structure, scene execution, characterization, and theme. When the major elements of story interact believably and smoothly, the story benefits.

A lot of recent urban fantasies follow a similar pattern. Powerful characters are often not quite what they seem to be. Many are shifters, more commonly known as shapeshifters, which readers are familiar with from books such as *Twilight* or from classic stories involving werewolves. Often these shifters are male and part of a love triangle with the female protagonist.

Urban fantasies and portal fantasies are often character-centric. The relationships and growth among the group or in comparison to the group of characters is important. In *Harry Potter*, the characters and the secondary world are often cited as the most interesting aspects of the story.

In Isaac Asimov's *I, Robot,* we are shown a world not unlike our own, but the robots have begun to take their place in the society, and so we see the unintended consequences of their integration. As a contrast, Asimov's *Prelude to Foundation* begins a journey into a huge and richly crafted future galaxy with ideas that still inspire fans of sci-fi to this day despite it being back in 1988.

You may be thinking: "Those examples are all well and good, but how do *I* do it?"

W riting Tip: Here are some actionable steps you can take to achieve your goals of building your urban fantasy world.

1) <u>Choose your genre</u> – Consider if you would enjoy writing a book about a fantasy race of shifter bears with a secret society in the mountains just outside a modern U.S. city. Do you love the idea of modern-day vampires? If some variation of this sounds appealing, I suggest starting there and figuring out what kind of shifter or creature you want to build around.

2) <u>Start with a detail</u> – Are your vampires solitary or part of a larger enclave? Does the secret society have a long-term goal? Usually, it does. Consider starting with a magical object like a wand or a sword. In C.S. Lewis's *The Chronicles of Narnia* series, the adventure begins with the children playing around in a wardrobe. The story starts in the real world, but the wardrobe is the portal through which the characters are transported into Lewis's secondary world.

In Carl Sagan's novel *Contact,* the alien signal is the trigger for the story to really begin. It's the first element that differentiates the story from our real-world experience as we've yet to confirm an alien signal on Earth.

3) <u>Derive a detail from a famous example</u> – Our world is full of many great examples that can be altered to great effect for your world-building needs. Ancient Rome, Imperial China, African kingdoms like Ethiopia and Egypt, Native American First Nations, and Meso-American ancient civilizations like the Incas, Mayans, or Aztecs can all be models for the world you want to write about. I would caution anyone looking to step outside their comfort zone and be more inclusive to do their research and have drafts looked over by people more knowledgeable on the culture, history, and traditions associated with that tradition.

How about a story in a world resembling dynastic China but with vampires? Or a world with a high-mountain kingdom like the Incas with dinosaurs? Or a dystopian America making all the wrong decisions with frightening technological advancements? The choices are endless.

4) <u>Urban fantasy is not epic fantasy or sci-fi.</u> Most of the examples in this book have come from the deep world-building inherent in works from those genres. We can all remember those huge door-stopper size books filled with every last detail the author could think of, but urban fantasy readers aren't necessarily gravitating toward stories that are heavy on world-building, so with that in mind, consider an important reason for each instance of world-building you include in your writing. We might not need to know the detailed aspects of your faerie colony's political structure or every bit of court intrigue.

CHAPTER 15

Food and Drink

One of my favorite aspects of world-building is certainly filling my stories with carefully chosen food and drinks. It's a brilliant way to show the kind of society you are portraying, but it also serves to add descriptive elements to your writing. Who doesn't like writing about delicious delicacies?

Some writers purposely add foods they think the reader will find repulsive or exotic to make a statement about the culture or characters. To give a classic example, in *Star Trek*, the Klingons eat a bowl of worms—often live worms—called "gagh" that is oddly similar to the English verb "gag", which is what many of us would do if faced with eating such a meal.

There are many varieties of these worms. One of the appeals to eating this Klingon delicacy is the way they feel when you swallow them. This dish is unpalatable for many humans of the Federation, and I believe the dish is used to make the Klingons seem even more exotic.

In *The Lord of the Rings*, the sweet drink known as Miruvor is a specialty of the elves and known to have restorative benefits. It was yet another element of world-building around the elves that made them seem mysterious and advanced.

In *A Song of Ice and Fire*, Daenerys Targaryen needs to eat the heart of a stallion during a divination ritual. The elites of the Dothraki Khalasar cheer her on as she valiantly finishes the humongous heart to the delight of her husband Khal Drogo. This was not only a moment of cultural custom but showed that the outsider Daenerys was resourceful enough to adapt to her surroundings—unlike her older brother Viserys Targaryen, who looked down on the Dothraki with contempt, eventually leading to his demise.

In the *Star Wars Universe*, I found their blue milk to be a simple but interesting inclusion, especially showing that the idea of milk was something common in even unrelated biological creatures from different star systems. The milk is produced by female banthas, but it showed up in a lot of different *Star Wars* media from novels, the comics, and on screen.

In *The Hitchhiker's Guide to the Galaxy*, we all remember the most powerful of beverages, Pan-Galactic Gargle Blaster. This wildly potent drink was known to cause drinkers to behave in funny and sometimes embarrassing ways.

In both *Foundation and Empire* and *The Evitable Conflict*, Robert Heinlein created interesting futuristic foods and beverages including flavored powder capsules that could be mixed with water to create a broad range of drinks. It is not entirely unlike

Kool-Aid powder, but still different enough to believe they would be used in a futuristic setting. Heinlein also created many yeast-based foods, perhaps most famously the yeast steak, which was comparably cheaper to produce than beef.

Vat-grown meat factored heavily in *The Neuromancer*'s advanced world where it was considered too expensive and wasteful to raise livestock just to eat.

In *Dune*, perhaps the most interesting of all sci-fi foods would have to be the spice melange. In truth, the spice was a type of bodily secretion of the great sand worms. A blue-glowing powder that was added to many foods, this drug was known to improve general health, increase the consumer's awareness of the world around them, and increase the length of one's lifespan, but it was highly addictive and sought the galaxy over. For some, it even helped unlock an ability called prescience that allowed for light-speed travel possibilities and was used by different factions in many incredible ways.

In the *Wayfarers* series by Becky Chambers, the humans of the future eat bugs. They are highly nutritious and take up little space compared to other food options. The idea of eating bugs has come up many times in scientific circles as a part of the eventual solution for sustainable subsistence, so it's nice to see sci-fi writers using it in their works.

In this excerpt from *Daughter of Dragons*, I add world-building into descriptions of the food to set the scene for a point-of-view character's memory of a feast.

"Queen Loli still remembered the magnificent spread her servants had prepared—roast pigs glazed with a sweet honey sauce and candied with bits of green apple; a thick, sour stew with fish caught from the high mountain lakes of the Red Dragon Mountains; white and brown breads of many varieties lined with rich creams and flakes of rare chocolate from the serif kingdom far to the east; roast lizard skewers covered in a spicy rub. The dishes kept coming out of the kitchens all evening and there were tall flagons of fine red wines spread across the long table."

I enjoy describing food in my books, and I think it's a nice way to add descriptive elements while also setting the scene. You can also add tidbits of world-building as I tried to do by including the Red Dragon Mountains and the serif kingdom as two places where the food had come from.

However you choose to do it, describing food and drink can add a unique touch to your story. Every writer who takes their time to select the foods and beverages they want to include will come up with something a bit different.

Here's to delicious writing!

CHAPTER 16

Use Your Senses

M ore to the point, let your readers use *their* senses. I touched very briefly on using sights and smells to give your locations added depth and a realism your readers can comfortably sink into. For a writer who values sparse details and wants to keep his world-building to the absolute minimum, very few smells, sights, and sounds are necessary. For those of us who want our locations to come to life, it's a good idea to let the reader experience these descriptive elements whenever they are of interest or whenever it can deepen the reader's experience.

W riting Tip: Try to avoid sacrificing pacing, plot, or characterization just to add elements of world-building. After all, if you are reading this book, you are likely writing genre fiction or perhaps preparing a well-crafted role-playing game session. Regardless of what you are writing, the world-building is always secondary to plot, characters, and pacing. Those are the three main elements of story that are absolutely essential. Elements of theme and description are powerful supporters of these elements, but it shouldn't work against them.

S mell is one of the most underused aspects of sense a writer should absolutely consider when describing how the point-of-view characters experience the world around them. I've heard many times that smell is the sense most-closely tied to memory and, some say, closely tied to our emotions.

We can include pleasant smells like those from fresh-baked pies, wildflowers, or spices like cinnamon, and link these smells to the elements of characterization and theme. How does the character feel when they walk by Grandma's window and smell fresh-baked cookies? Do they drop their pretenses and display child-like joy as they rush to gobble up the cookies before they get cold? Do they fail to react, perhaps invoking a surprised reaction from Granny? Their reaction can reveal that something is bothering the character, who would otherwise be delighted by the chance to eat the cookies or at least enjoy the passing scent.

A character walks into a dark, peaceful temple and is greeted by the welcoming soft fragrance of incense. How will that make her feel? Will it trigger an important memory? Will it give the reader a deeper experience as we travel with the character through the temple?

We don't need to write about scents as well as Marcel Proust or James Joyce to get a lot out of the skill. You can try the basic techniques below if you are having trouble with adding elements of scent to your work. "The scent of ____ greeted her as she entered the ____." or "The place stank of ___ and ___."

A nother instructive example of using fragrance in writing is George R. R. Martin's use of smells along with sights as he describes the food people are eating, from the basic bowl o' brown sold in roadside inns and all throughout FleaBottom to the multi-course banquets served in the dining halls of locations such as Winterfell and the Red Keep.

Martin sets up clues to the scene based on what kind of food is available to the point-of-view character, whether this food meets their expectations or standards, whether this food is even allowed to be eaten, as in the case of the captive Theon Greyjoy, or whether the characters are even interested in the food, which often suggests they have more pressing matters to think about despite their nostrils telling them it's time to eat.

We can also include nasty smells to great effect as anyone who has read horror or hard crime-scene investigation stories already knows all too well.

In *The Inquisitor*, I wrote: "Something dark flew past his head, splattering against the cracked wall of his cell . . . the stench gave him the answer before he saw it.

Shit.

Streaks of brown—courtesy of one of his neighbors in the next cell—were already giving off a vomit-inducing stink. Nestor grabbed his wash rag and covered his mouth and nose; it was all he could do to keep from losing his breakfast."

It's useful to include sensations for the reader to imagine because it gives that dungeon depth and realism. It also allows you to use characterization. How does the character deal with the terrible smell? He can't leave the cell. How will he treat the neighboring prisoners who are making his cell even more hellish than it already is? The nasty smell, and perhaps the visual image of the dungeon scene, made all of those opportunities possible.

Including nasty smells into your story can be effective in drawing a reader in, but it's important to know where to draw the line. Being gross for the sake of it could lead to readers flipping past the scene or putting the book down. As with most aspects of writing, there is a balance.

Sounds are often incorporated to change scenes or quicken the pace. In horror movies, the most common example is the jump scare. It could be a loud or sudden noise, often a scream, or motion across the screen like a cat knocking down cans in an alley. The jump scare seeks to relieve the building pressure with a payoff of sorts. It can also be used as a moment for an unjustified sigh of relief by both the viewer and character before the real danger reveals itself.

Of course, it's much more challenging to present sounds in as effective a way as scriptwriters can through cinema. Outside of audiobooks, our medium is generally silent, so how does one convey a feeling of sound from the act of reading? It's an interesting question.

With sound, we are often best off letting the reader take over without being too descriptive. In the past, my editors often told me a sentence needed to be rewritten because the descriptions of the sounds were too jarring or long-winded. At the time, I didn't consider that sounds are often experienced momentarily. Spending half a paragraph to get the descriptive "just right" was often "just wrong".

We should seek word choices that help sounds flow into our sentences. This dips into the old advice of "show don't tell", but it's often better just to use stronger action verbs instead of convoluted attempts to describe sounds—which I have been very guilty of.

The roaring fire, a character gasping, liquid dripping, and birds singing are all quite natural ways to represent the sounds of your world as the characters move through it. Some words that have worked for me to help build the sounds around my characters include soft, sweet, rhythmic, deafening, thunderous, and shrill.

Don't be afraid to use onomatopoeia when it works, but try not to go as far as comic books. Comic books are able to make use of the visual space on the page in ways we novelists cannot. Some examples of appropriate onomatopoeia would be words like growl, moan, creak, whisper, squeal, and pop. There are, of course, many more. I recommend browsing through lists online for appropriate onomatopoeia that will work in your given descriptions.

The thesaurus is another friend when trying to enlarge your lexicon of words or just to get a broader understanding of the links between a matrix of words that share similar meanings or usage. If you find yourself using the same descriptives throughout your manuscript, I urge you to look at synonyms for that word so that you aren't boring your readers with everything being "big" or "sweet".

Sight remains the most useful sense we can use in our world-building. If a writer focuses on a small handful of visual details and carefully brings them to life, the reader can fill in the blanks and imagine the rest for themselves, which allows you to move on to the plot, dialogue, and characterizations of the scene. The caveat is that the few details you give need to be top-notch, using the best possible adjectives to build truly evocative sentences.

In *The Lord of the Rings: The Fellowship of the Rings* by J.R.R. Tolkien, we are given this impressive description of Elrond.

"The face of Elrond was ageless, neither old nor young, though in it was written the memory of many things both glad and sorrowful. His hair was dark as the shadows of twilight, and upon it was set a circlet of silver; his eyes were grey as a clear evening, and in them was a light like the light of stars."

Very little of that description forces anything concretely onto the reader's visual impression of Elrond beyond the dark hair and grey eyes, but we feel satisfied with the description. This gives us some agency in the story as we can use our imagination to fill in how we perceive Elrond. Tolkien's visual cues are fascinating and beautiful without feeling like a restriction on the imagination of the reader. We are still free to explore our own interpretations of Elrond.

Here is a brief description from *Dune* of the protagonist Paul Atreides.

"A smile touched Paul's mouth, but there was a hardness in the expression that reminded Gurney of the Old Duke, Paul's grandfather. Gurney saw then the sinewy harshness in Paul that had never before been seen in an Atreides—a leathery look to the skin . . ."

A hardness in Paul's smile. A sinewy harshness. A leathery look to the skin. All great descriptions that don't bind us too tightly as we explore our own impression of the protagonist through the eyes of another character. The sight of Paul and how Gurney reacts to his appearance reveals more about Gurney than it does about Paul, though it does give some sense that Paul has been through things a privileged member of a royal house seldom has to go through.

One of the first things I noticed back when I was starting my writing journey came from my experiences trading chapters and scenes in online writing groups. Many of the other writers I swapped unedited work with had similar descriptive problems when trying to give visual world-building clues to the reader. There were many variants of this when a new character—or even one the reader had come across many times before—entered the scene.

1) "Jane Johnson entered the room. She had blue eyes and long straight brown hair."

2) "Bob Brown's eyes were an ocean blue. He had cropped black hair and a warm smile."

3) "Mira's eyebrows raised as Kira Kirakirason sat down beside her. Kira's curly red hair stopped just above her shoulders and complemented her mysterious green eyes."

I hope you've noticed the pattern here. There seemed to be an unwritten rule among amateur writers that when a new character entered the scene, we needed details about their eye color and hair. Over and over again, I saw examples of this! So much so, that I assumed it must have been part of the common writing practice. Later, I realized that these writers didn't know their characters because they hadn't developed a backstory for them. It's much easier to describe your characters if you know things like what they do for a living, how old they are, their hobbies, etc.

This crosses over into the world-building realm even though the descriptions are an element of characterization, because the writer seems unable to reveal anything interesting about the character.

If I know that this character just came from the gym, I can then create a much better description. I can mention the casual after-gym clothing. Or the gym bag they are toting, or the sweat on their brow. If I know that they are an office worker who works long hours, I can present them with clothing, attitude, and expressions that blend in with the world-building to tell the reader more than just hair and eye color.

Personally, I rarely notice someone's eye color when they walk into a room or when I first meet them. It might not be true for you, but I think as writers we can do better than this. I've put down more than a few stories that take characterization for granted. If they had just written down a few aspects of the character's background—a few minutes of well-spent world-building—their stories would be much easier to delve into.

T aste is easy!

Rarely have I read a book where taste was an issue. For whatever reason, maybe we are just good at describing taste because—besides certain aspects of touch—taste is often the most strongly noticed aspect of sense. Some people might not notice a bad smell, a remarkable sight, a strange sound, or an odd sensation, but it's hard for someone not to notice the spicy peppers in the dish they are eating.

If you are someone who has trouble describing taste, the good news is that this is easily fixable. Less is often more. You don't need to tell us much more about the steak besides that it smelled good and tasted better! A similar description is often enough for readers. We can easily imagine a tasty pizza or bowl of ice cream.

There is no reason to redefine what vanilla or pepperoni tastes like to the character.

F inally, touch.

This is the one that can often make or break a scene. Sadly, there isn't a tremendous amount that world-building can do about that. Touch is much more clearly located in the characterization section of the Venn diagram. Learning good description of touch is a bit outside the scope of this book. The best advice I can give as a writer who struggles with describing this sense is to give you the often-quoted advice of "read widely in the genre in which you wish to write".

That's right. And take notes. Take notes of every sensual scene. Make notes about the parts that appealed to you and the parts you found jarring or forgettable. During a fight scene, do the descriptions make sense? Are the actions possible or realistic? How do they describe the feeling of pain?

Stepping back into more general questions, how do they describe hot and cold? Rough and soft? Wet and dry? Again, these aren't really world-building questions, and we have to really think hard to make them such, but I think it's important to consider all five aspects of sense to create more believable writing.

W riting Tip: Create sheets with basic information about your characters. These character sheets can be informal notes about physical traits, basics on motivations, and a list of the conflicts the characters have with each other. Be sure to include aspects of world-building to the characters like economic status—poor or rich—education level, age, occupation, wants, desires, and goals. Strengths and weakness are perhaps the most important of these details to really flesh out.

CHAPTER 17

Cartography and the Art of Map-Making

You've got an amazing story all ready to go, but you want to go the extra mile to give your readers something else to dig in to. What can you do?

Well, one important consideration is a map. You've gone to all the effort to develop a world full of interesting races, kingdoms, and amazing geographical features. Why not show it off?

Whether it's a galactic map for your epic space opera, a world map for your quest fantasy, or a city map for your murder mystery, a map can go a long way toward impressing the reader and helping them become immersed in your story.

Called *mappa mundi* in Latin, the early world maps of Europe still interest historians and world-builders for their unique characteristics. World maps were mysterious pieces of knowledge in the past. All the empty or unfilled space on the ancient maps—known as *terra incognita*—inspired writers and philosophers for ages to speculate what interesting lands, people, animals, and monsters were hidden behind the veil.

If I'm not making myself clear yet, less is often more. Leaving some mysterious unexplored areas on your own map gives the reader leave to consider their own ideas of what might exist around the next corner or just over the horizon. It also gives you opportunities to travel to those areas during your stories. Ancient maps were much less concerned with exact scales of size, as many factors of measurement were still in doubt during those times. You might warp the actual size of things on your map to reflect the feelings of *your* mapmaker.

Perhaps there are many scary stories of conquest about the people to the north, so their land is depicted as vast—hence their strength as conquerors, and perhaps with harsh environments, because why would people with lush resources focus on warfare? You can drop those ideas on their head by having some of your characters visit this "scary" land only to find out it isn't quite what the mapmakers and historians had made it out to be.

There are quite a few benefits to trying your hand at a map—or hiring out your idea to a talented creative.

Fantasy and sci-fi readers seem to love maps. Think about that most famous of fantasy maps of Middle-earth from *The Lord of the Rings* or the map of Westeros and Essos from *A Song of Ice and Fire*. These are some of the most iconic pieces of fantasy ever to grace a page. Remember in *The Hobbit*, Bilbo Baggins making his way to the Misty Mountains with tales of Smaug to terrify him with every step closer he took.

Maps also force you to be more aware of the locations you are writing about. How close are your characters to the sea? You can take a look at the map and make decisions on how likely it would be for fresh fish to arrive at their landlocked kingdom that's a week by horse to the nearest sea.

Checking your map can help you to figure out where to place a forest. You can confidently create lush greeneries around big rivers and in low-lying valleys where many smaller streams flow to from snow-capped peaks far away. I recommend making the map first before selecting all the locations for the story, otherwise, you might end up making unbelievable loca- tions and "stretching" things because you've already plotted out that river running through the desert with no trees anywhere to be seen.

I can't tell you how many unbelievable maps I've seen on social media where simple environmental factors are forgotten to create an unbelievable set of locations for the plot. Do better!

Maps are a convention that lends a certain sense of credibility to the author. When I open a book by an author I'm not familiar with and see a well-crafted and intriguing map, I am relieved and happy. In indie publishing, one of the key maxims for gaining readership is: Cover, blurb, look inside.

The cover attracts the reader's eye as they scroll through pages online or flip through paperbacks in a brick-and-mortar bookstore; the blurb or back cover copy is the enticing glimpse into what the book has to offer and should lead potential readers to look inside.

For fantasy and sci-fi writers, adding a fourth part—the epic map —can also help to gain new readers.

Not only that, but maps are loads of fun to create.

Full disclosure, I'm terrible at drawing, handwriting, and visual arts in general. The idea of making a fantasy map was nightmarish for me. Luckily, I have a graphic designer in the family and the world map in my *Daughter of Havenglade* series and my Pax Grati city map in *The Inquisitor* were made sense of by said family member from my chicken scratch notes.

For my current project, I went online and decided to try mapmaking myself. Not because I planned to include my version of the world map in my final project, but because I wanted to use the map to world-build and plot things out. I plan on having the map professionally done, but even the worst of us visual-arts types can still get it done with software like Inkarnate or, if you are more artistically inclined, *Photoshop*.

W riting Tip: What not to do. Don't make the map fit the story when not absolutely necessary. Create the map before you make the story or create multiple maps and pick the map that's best suited to your story. There is no reason to have readers criticize bad map-making decisions because the writer failed to make a believable map.

CHAPTER 18

How To Build Histories

E ven for hard-core world-builders, the thought of writing out a detailed history for the world and story they plan to write lends to fears of eyes glazing over and of a life wasted writing about minutiae that will likely never make it into the story.

I think it's important to address these fears and to know what kind of options are likely to lead a writer down the best path when writing anything related to a world history.

First off, what do we mean by a story history?

I usually think of it as working through and writing out the events from the past—both recent and distant—which affect the characters' thoughts and actions during the story.

I n *A Game of Thrones*, the characters are deeply affected by many complicated events throughout both their personal histories and the history of the Seven Kingdoms.

King Robert Baratheon has a strong relationship with Ned Stark, not in small part based on the deeply troubling past they both have lived through. During Robert's Rebellion, the Baratheons, Starks, and several other major houses led a rebellion against the ruling Targaryens. There is a lot of deeper conflict from hundreds of years prior when the Targaryens invaded Westeros, but I will focus on the more recent history that drives Robert Baratheon and Ned Stark for now.

This conflict was partially triggered by Ned's father and older brother being killed by the Mad King and the assumption that Prince Rhaegar Targaryen had kidnapped Ned Stark's sister Lyanna Stark, who was betrothed to Robert Baratheon at the time.

It's a beautiful and tragic history that I encourage you to look into if you want to learn more about the *A Song of Ice and Fire* backstory. These traumatic events from the past help to shape the bonds of loyalty and feelings of unease between characters who were on the right or wrong side of the war.

The good news is that we don't need to create hundreds of pages of history to create believable fantasy or sci-fi. I personally write out some notes on history when I realize the characters need it. For example, in my *Daughter of Havenglade* series, I wanted the primary antagonist Queen Loli to be less of a purely evil villain and started giving her some backstory in point-of-view chapters in *Blood Cauldron* and *Daughter of Dragons*. More than a few readers have noted that they started liking her more and more as the series came to its end, even though they knew she had to be stopped.

Your history doesn't have to be written out on the page or delivered as information dumps. I believe first and foremost that world-building histories serve to help add depth to the characters, conflicts, and culture of your story. If you, the writer, know what happened in the past, you can employ the effects of those events into the present of your adventure.

It's not enough that your peasants live under blistering taxes. Was there ever an uprising? Perhaps a character lost a loved one during the conflict and now distrusts officials more than the average peasant. She has a real bone to pick, but as the writer, you hold back the reason for a time. We just see her bump heads and act particularly fierce toward the local tax collector until, at the perfect moment, we find out it's not just the unjust tax rate but the loss of life that has shaped her rage.

In *The Inquisitor*, my protagonist Nestor Atias is shaped by a complex personal history. He came to live in a foreign land when he was very young. He is one of the few black faces in the city. People have treated him and his family quite differently, but in particular, his father was driven out of business by a wealthy local who wanted to corner the market on certain trade goods. This destroyed Nestor's family and led him to taking the extreme step of joining the local monastic order and becoming a monk (and an inquisitor). He didn't join for the right reasons and things fell apart.

I present these important bits of personal history throughout the story as they seem most relevant. But since I don't want it to slow down the narrative, I pick spots where I feel it works best.

For one of my works in progress, I have a notebook of about forty pages of notes on history and world-building. I've done it because I enjoy it, but I know it will give my series tons of depth because the characters, locations, and conflicts have so much depth.

I've created multiple constructed languages from scratch, just so I can use a couple of dozen words and phrases. Now, I'm not suggesting anyone needs to follow in my footsteps. In fact, you absolutely don't need to, but I love my stories that much and really want to give them all I can in terms of depth and a life of their own.

One of the most important events from the past that I've created for my current work in progress is the history of the settlers slowly pushing the locals from their homelands until a great war broke out. This concept is nothing new, but it serves the purposes of my story to have characters whose families came from both sides of this conflict and have different world views and ideas about these historical events.

Great victories or genocides? Depends on who wrote the history, of course. And when these characters collide, everyone is forced to consider if the narratives they've been taught since their youth are as true as they've always been led to believe.

Writing Tip: Write your history as you go. When you realize your characters or conflict will benefit more from a less superficial conflict, take the time to give it the depth it deserves. People are motivated by their worldview and their world views are shaped by culture, history, and relationships. Help your characters gain depth through world-building personal and collective histories, and they will return the favor by giving you amazing performances in your writing.

CHAPTER 19

More on Magic Systems

I touched on magical systems earlier in the book, but let's face it, having the right magic system can make or break your story. People read fantasy in part for the sense of wonder found in the magic. What's possible in your world that isn't in ours? That's the beauty of fantasy, and of sci-fi, where the "magic" is future technology and alien lifeforms, but more on that later.

I also wrote about why giving your magic limitations is important. To put a period on that conversation, don't be the writer who gives your characters god-like powers with such minor drawbacks as to be inconsequential.

I've read stories where the protagonist is basically an invulnerable Superman and the only drawback was that he couldn't remember his past . . . yet he remembers what he needs to know for the plot and the story whenever necessary. I've read a story where a witch could control anyone's mind within eyesight and the only drawback was a feeling of weakness and a headache.

Create stakes and conflict between your characters and the magic system. Either there are serious consequences the character must consider when using magic, or the magic is weaker, and we are left wondering if the magic will be enough to solve the problems the protagonist faces.

From where does the magic spring forth?

Is it a dark magic which comes from blood sacrifice? This magical trope works well for villains but can be subverted to make a "goody" more morally gray. Perhaps the hero knows using blood magic is forbidden, but they make a choice to use the taboo arts once to do something they think is just. Of course, there must be harsh consequences for their actions. This is what makes for a good story.

Blood magic involves the spilling of blood or the act of killing during a magical ritual. Sometimes the blood must be drunk, sometimes there is a bloodbath or another equally gruesome display. It's common for the blood to have specific requirements. In *A Song of Ice and Fire*, the Red Woman, Melisandre, requires royal blood for her visions and spells. As you can imagine, virgin blood is a common trope. There is often a corrupting element to blood magic. Those who partake are less themselves over time or suffer some physical maladies. Blood magic is an interesting, if not overdone, magical system to consider for your world-building.

Not far from blood magic is necromancy. Necromancy deals with the dark art of raising the dead. Whether it's an army of bear skeletons or zombie werewolves, this magic almost always falls on the evil side as it is seen as robbing the dead of their rest and controlling their bodies without their permission.

Zombies lead to images of rot, decay, and corruption, which are generally not going to make people like the necromancer. Sometimes necromancers might simply commune with the dead or bring a corpse back to life to ask a few questions. Necromancers, like practitioners of blood magic, often have found unnatural ways to extend their lives, giving them an appearance of youth that often fades away to reveal the truth.

Crystal-based magical systems are also quite popular because of their ease of use and the sense of wonder within the mysterious stones. Sometimes the magic users derive all of their power from the crystals, sometimes the crystal combines with a magically inclined individual to create a wizard. These crystals tend to be rare or well-guarded to keep this power from slipping into the wrong hands or even to keep it away from the peasantry so the ruling elites can maintain their power.

Another way to express the magic in your world is through spell books. Everyone can use magic, if they know the right incantation or have the right ingredients. Spells and potions become a type of misunderstood technology that anyone can call upon if they learn the methods.

In spell-book stories, the magical arts are kept by secret societies so as to deny the rest of the world the chance to use—or abuse—magic. Many witch and shifter stories revolve around these secret societies.

Whatever magic system you come up with has to interest you as the writer. Don't just peg yourself into one of the methods without considering whether you'll enjoy writing about it. If it doesn't interest you, you won't garner much interest from your readers.

Switching gears to sci-fi, the magic is the future technology inherent in your world. Light-speed travel, teleporting, and laser weapons are common examples. Some technologies are aesthetic world-building, which add little to the plot—think food replicators that are mentioned in passing just to show the technological level of the society.

Other technologies, like a time machine, might have much more serious plot implications. It's important that the writer create a technology that will be central to the plot. The Death Star from *Star Wars*, red matter from *Star Trek*, and avatars from Avatar are all examples of technology that figure in to the central plot.

Consider showing the negative consequences of powerful technologies in unique ways. The people of the future have wonderful technology, yet they still live troubled lives and things aren't what the reader might imagine the future to be like.

Who is trying to exploit a noble and worthy tech for their own benefit? Perhaps the tech isn't as great as it's made out to be, or it might even be a fiendishly devised trap and not a boon for society at all. Event Horizon, anyone?

Writing Tip: It's fine to have many aesthetic technologies in your story but make sure you have a central technology that the plot depends on. This is an element that separates sci-fi from other genres and ensures that it's not just a story about gadgets of the future. What are the stakes? What are the risks technology poses to your characters?

CHAPTER 20

Future Technology

For those of us writing sci-fi as opposed to fantasy, the magic system is the future technology present in our worlds. Arthur C. Clarke famously posited that "Any sufficiently advanced technology is indistinguishable from magic." This is the premise around which we can world-build our sci-fi stories. Capture the fascination and wonder of magic through the lens of science and plausible tools in the future.

We will look at a few of the most popular technologies that exist in both hard and soft sci-fi, but writers shouldn't feel pigeonholed into using a trope just for the sake of it. Think which technology will inspire you to write the best, most interesting story possible.

Time travel is one of the most popular tropes in sci-fi. Starting way back in 1895 with H.G. Wells's classic *The Time Machine*, the idea of time travel has fascinated us ever since. Who wouldn't want to travel to the past to fix a huge mistake or go to the future just to see what life was like? Wells explores a bizarre future and takes his time traveler on an interesting journey before he can return back to the comforts of his own time.

James Cameron's *Terminator* franchise takes a unique approach to using technology world-building as a main attraction. An artificial intelligence in the future has destroyed civilization as we know it, but a hero is about to help humans turn the tide and defeat the robots, so the robots use a newly invented time machine to send a killer robot back in time to kill the hero—John Connor—before he's born. By killing Sarah Connor—John Connor will never lead the resistance against the robots.

As luck would have it, the humans are able to send back a defender to help Sarah Connor stay safe from the terminator. This world-building involves a plot which takes place during "our time" but the premise is from the future and employs time travel to the past.

In Michael Crichton's novel *Sphere*, a mysterious craft, which appears to have been sent back in time more than three hundred years ago, must be explored and the alien technology within tests the explorers to their limits. Time-travel technology in this story merely serves as a device to get the object to "our time" and doesn't seem to serve a large purpose to the plot other than giving the alien sphere a more plausible origin and making the origins of the craft more mysterious.

In Stephen King's *11/22/63*, an everyman character is given an opportunity to travel through a portal back to the year 1958. A dying friend then asks him to do a big thing. To live in the past until November 22, 1963 and prepare to stop Lee Harvey Oswald from killing JFK. It's a fascinating take on the time portal trope.

Another staple of sci-fi technology is faster-than-light travel, commonly known as light-speed travel. This future technology is so ubiquitous that it's surprising to come across a story that doesn't take advantage of this technology. Why? Well, objects in outer space are far apart from each other. I mean very far apart. Discounting our sun, the next closest star to Earth is Alpha Centauri. A mind-boggling 4.37 light years from the Sun.

That means, if you were traveling at the speed of light—approximately 300,000 km per second—it would take almost four-and-a-half years nonstop. Sci-fi writers are imaginative and far-reaching writers. They don't just want to go to Alpha Centauri. They want to travel across the Milky Way Galaxy or to other galaxies. When you think of it that way, it's almost impossible not to deal with travel time in space. But if you don't want to go the time-travel route, the story would be about traveling between stars, which could be an interesting take.

Many sci-fi stories deal with travel more directly and make it an element of plot or part of the high concept. Dune incorporates a Holtzman Drive to fold space-time in a way that makes places much more accessible, but Frank Herbert wasn't done there. To make it all work, another important aspect of his world-building and plot—the spice melange was incorporated. A pilot of a Holtzman Drive would need to be high on the spice or they could never navigate through space-time safely—two technological bits of world-building that are central to the story of Dune.

The most obvious example of this technology-driven a plot is, of course, *Stargate*. The entire franchise is based on these portals, which are essentially Einstein-Rosen Bridges, known more commonly as wormholes. The Stargate found in Egypt happens to lead them to a world of slaves dominated by powerful alien beings posing as gods.

Whether you use actual faster-than-light travel like *Star Trek's* Warp Drive, a Holtzman Drive, or a wormhole, consider whether this will be a feature technology you can build a plot around, or if it's just a matter of interstellar convenience.

You could build your future tech around the threat of a doomsday device. Known synonymously with the big red button, a doomsday device is a type of weapon or weaponized piece of scientific equipment that could destroy the starship, planet, galaxy, you name it.

I advise against going the mad scientist route as it's been done to death, but if you have a fresh angle, don't let me stand in your way. These days, more often than not, a well-meaning but blind-sided genius creates or wields the doomsday device and has the readers on the edge of their lounge chairs wondering if this is going to be the end of things.

The most glaring example is the Death Star from *Star Wars*. The Death Star is an orbital station with the ability to destroy entire planets. But we have other prime examples like the Little Doctor device in *Ender's Game* and *The Hitchhiker's Guide to the Galaxy* which features Hactar's Ultimate Weapon, a linkage of interstellar warps which bind together every sun threatening to destroy them all.

Be careful that your incredibly dangerous device isn't merely a shiny McGuffin. Many sci-fi stories and graphic novels depend upon these devices to drive the entire plot, and then at the end they are averted, meaning the device sat there looking scary for the entire story. Also, the villain wielding a doomsday device is prone to becoming one-dimensional and caring about nothing but activating the device.

What kind of unique technology are you most interested in building for your world? There is still much new ground to be broken in this aspect of world-building. With a bit of thoughtful outlining, any talented writer could give us a new angle on future technologies that doesn't just serve to drive the plot but also makes us think about contemporary issues and problems that get their world-building tentacles linked into theme. Whenever your world-building is interwoven with theme, you have something truly special.

CHAPTER 21

Military Logistics

Depending on your story, you may need to describe a large army or even a small band of traveling soldiers. There are some stark differences in the way some writers go about writing the details of military logistics. The term itself sounds daunting. Most of us aren't generals, some of us may have a military background or experience with supply chains—which is more important than you might have thought—but we all could stand to learn more on this subject.

Why should we describe military logistics at all? That's a good question considering some writers include inaccurate details or choose to gloss over them completely, so as to avoid the inaccurate details and the time spent learning about military logistics.

What I'm suggesting is not akin to enrolling at West Point to become a strategist. I'm suggesting looking into a few basic details that will make it look like you've looked into everything. With a few well-placed details—that check out upon a search—you can let the leader believe your real-world details so they can suspend their disbelief of the fantastic details like fire-breathing dragons and inertial dampeners.

The other point I will be referencing over and over again in this chapter is that by including details about the logistics in your world-building, it will naturally lead to opportunities for character development, establishing and ramping up conflicts, and even for theme to present itself. One of the main takeaways from this book should be that world-building compliments and adds to the story. It isn't something outside of the story like an information dump.

So, while we are here, let's look at a few considerations in military logistics. Keep in mind that I am in no way an expert. These are merely suggestions and examples. It's up to you how deep you want to go. I certainly expect many writers reading this book will create much better examples of world-building than I ever will, and the idea of that delights me.

How are soldiers and supplies transported?

Whether they travel by carts, wagons, ships, or even on the backs of fantastic beasts, every fantasy writer who wishes to make their military descriptions as believable as possible needs to consider the basic necessities of such travel methods.

What will the transport be carrying? Only soldiers? What about their supplies? Won't they need to bring food? Weapons? Equipment?

In the case of carts or wagons, the size of the transport largely determines what can be carried. If peasants are pulling the carts, the contents will need to be much lighter. If you use horses, then the contents can be heavier, and if you use a yoke of oxen, the cargo can be even heavier, but those beasts of burden need to eat often and not just the wild grasses along the side of the trade route. That's lazy writing. Horses won't stay healthy for long without a more nutritious diet. Consider the grains and even a small amount of fruits and vegetables for the pack animals to keep them healthy and happy.

Again, this leads to conflict and elements of story. What if halfway to their destination, the army runs out of feed? The travel conditions are tough and some of the animals start getting weak. Characters argue about what to do about this problem, which can lead to interesting conflicts.

It's fun to create an army, twenty-thousand strong, marching across the realm to siege an enemy stronghold or meet them on the field of battle, but hardened fantasy readers will consider how far the army is traveling by taking a look at your spiffy world map and get pulled right out of the story when they realize the army is marching a thousand kilometers in just a few days, in heavy rain, with no mention of supplies.

And yes, this crops up all the time. Often readers forgive them—if they are famous authors—but sometimes they don't, and the book reviews suffer from it. No need to give readers more reason to say your story was unrealistic. I know what you are saying right now as you read this. "But it's a fantasy novel. If they can accept the inherent elements of impossibility like magic, spells, horrid monsters, etc. surely, they can accept some loose details in other parts of the book?"

Well, no . . . the firm handling of the world-building allows them permission to suspend disbelief in the fantasy elements. It's an unspoken pact between the writer and the reader.

Perhaps your army is being transported on ships. You might think there's no need to feed draft animals or bring along a small force of servants and squires to take care of the day-to-day grunt work of wartime travel, but you would be wrong.

It's not at all out of the question to carry along horses if they will be an asset once the army makes landfall. If your army will be fighting a battle on the open field, they would likely want to have cavalry units because they will surely face cavalry units from a formidable enemy, but if the seas are too rough, the journey too long, or you just don't want to transport pack animals and the like, that's fine.

While it's certainly true that traveling by sea is a smart way to save time—and therefore supplies—in many fantasy settings, there are also world-building problems to solve on the high seas.

Assuming you have fair weather, sound vessels, competent navigators, and accurate maps, you'll want to highlight some technical aspects of the journey to make it real for the reader.

Obviously, these are also opportunities for elements of plot and character conflict as some of these things often go wrong in real-life and in fiction.

What type of ships make up your fleet? How many crew and passengers can each ship comfortably hold? If they are packed like sardines, that could lead to some interesting dialogue and some resentment from the lower ranks.

Your twenty thousand soldiers would require a fleet the size of which perhaps hasn't been seen in your world before. The trireme is a popular choice based on its speed, naval prowess, and sleek construction. Built for speed, triremes wouldn't be carrying much in the way of supplies. They could hold up to two hundred crew of which about one-hundred-and-sixty might need to be oarsman. There were sometimes up to eighty oars.

That would be about one hundred triremes for twenty thousand soldiers—let's say one-hundred-and-twenty for good measure, and that doesn't include larger and smaller vessels needed to transport food, supplies, sailors, generals, servants, squires and the like.

Perhaps the fleet could be led by three mighty flagships—galleons. Your armada of triremes would be a sight to see as they came in off the enemy's coast but the real big ships would be the galleons. Who's to say your civilization didn't develop huge powerful ships early on in their history? Minus the cannons, of course. These mighty warships were quite stable even in rough waters and depended on greatly reduced wind resistance, which made the ships fast and easier to maneuver than other large vessels—google search "galleons" for a detailed explanation of their construction.

Galleons reached up to two thousand tons and were excellent choices both for transport and as warships. The amount of work that went in to construct these ships was truly incredible. From blacksmiths to coopers, carpenters to shipwrights, pitch melters to engineers, many specialists labored on these amazing ships. Of course, knowing this could easily lead to some character creation.

Perhaps the general is pressuring the lead engineer to finish the ships faster, and this engineer knows they may have to compromise the ship's proper construction to fulfill the general's request for a quickly produced ship. In this way, your minor world-building gives you ideas for new characters, new conflict, and new elements of plot. That certainly seems like a good reason to do a little world-building.

Be sure to estimate the distance your fleet needs to travel, and set a reasonable estimate for how far the ships will sail each day. This will tell you how many days your fleet will need to travel on the sea—barring unforeseen events . . . which we all know could never happen in a fantasy novel.

So, twenty thousand soldiers plus another two or three thousand logistical hands—the unseen heroes of ancient warfare. A crew of approximately three hundred per galleon, and twenty-five crew per cog—cogs are a good "filler" ship that was relatively inexpensive to build and spacious for a smaller ship. Three of these galleons plus about thirty cogs could round out the rest of your armada, complementing the one-hundred-and-twenty triremes carrying the bulk of the fighting force.

The endless ships sailing across the open sea would be amazing to watch from the shore, and terrifying to watch from the enemy's castle as the vast number of hostile ships approached for an imminent attack.

Of course, this is only one possible way to build a fleet. There are likely much better ways to do it, but since I'm not an expert on naval strategy, I did my best to research a few key elements and built off those. Try researching different maritime technology from cultures and countries you are unfamiliar with. This is a great way to stumble across interesting things you never knew about before.

Even a small patrol of twenty scouts on horseback should be properly provisioned. Fill those saddlebags!

Writing Tip: The idea behind world-building mundane details, like travel supplies, isn't just to make you sound like a clever writer. First, if you can make the normal details accurate and well-defined, the reader can more easily suspend their disbelief of the fantasy elements like dragons and wizards. Second, dealing with the little problems and logistics of essential provisioning gives you ample opportunities to create conflict between characters and add depth to the journey.

In science fiction, it's often less difficult to plan the major logistics as so many stories have warp drives, cold fusion reactors, Dyson spheres, and various other futuristic technologies that explain away problems such as distance, energy, and capacity.

But what happens when the enemy has more advanced technology, so that a conventional attack would be suicidal? Sci-fi military transportation can include strategy and tactics about how the star fleet will outsmart or outclass their enemies.

For example, the Romulans and the Klingons—two alien species in the *Star Trek Universe*—have starship-cloaking devices that create an energy shield which can render their vessels almost invisible to sensors. Perhaps, that could lead to a planetary system with strange physical properties that make the cloaking devices useless.

The knowledge that the enemy has such a powerful tactical ability must be taken into account in all battle plans involving species with advanced technologies.

In *The Return of the Jedi*, the Rebellion must overcome the Empire's military superiority, culminating in a strategy to disable the Death Star's defense shields and exploiting a tactical weakness in the Death Star's design.

Writing Tip: It can be fun to give the protagonist's fleet a lot of flashy and powerful technology, but many of the most interesting stories involving sci-fi military encounters include overcoming long odds—which creates tension in the plot. It's like the Superman problem. Often, it's difficult to create tension in plots involving Superman because the writers need to somehow create a plot where Superman could lose, but that's hard to do because you need to either create outrageously powerful antagonists or rehash another kryptonite story.

Starting at a more reasonable level for both your technology and protagonists allows them room to grow and a place for them to be—at least temporarily—outclassed by the antagonist.

In both *Star Trek* and *Star Wars*, even the most amazing, advanced starships constantly break down with some sort of mechanical issues the crews have to solve or have their design pushed past their known limits. Think Han Solo working on the Millennium Falcon or Scotty pushing the U.S.S. Enterprise's warp drive past its limits.

Even if you are writing your story through the trope of shiny-looking spacecraft where the vessels all have spotless interiors and everything looks futuristic sleek and clean, you can still set-up logistical military and transport problems for your characters to deal with. A fair number of stories base a large part of the plot on a mysterious problem with the ship, sometimes caused by a rogue crew member or some strange cosmic phenomenon. An example of this is the problems that arise in *2001: A Space Odyssey* or the entire premise of the *Sliders* sci-fi television series.

A quick word of advice for writers who think their army will just "live off of the land", pillaging as they march toward their enemy's stronghold. A common strategy throughout ancient history was for an enemy to destroy their own crops and remove everything of value before the enemy arrived. These drastic measures include burning supplies and anything useful that couldn't be packed off, to ensure they wouldn't be feeding their enemy.

An army counting on this strategy would find itself marching home with its tail between its legs, with no supplies and no way to feed its soldiers. Of course, this could be used to show that a general is foolhardy and reckless. Do with it what you will.

W ho is financing the military campaign? A single monarch? Several rich and powerful lords? Perhaps an artificial intelligence, if you're writing sci-fi. It might be interesting to write a secondary motivation into the financier's reasoning for accepting the expenses of a costly military campaign into your world-building/character history. This motivation could be unknown to the point-of-view characters, therefore creating some surprises later. Perhaps the characters know about the secondary motivations and do something with that information. Either way, it adds depth to the reasons for going to war and gives your characters a sense of realism they might otherwise lack as just a prop character with deep pockets.

Now, let's consider something unrelated that may provide a parallel. The magic systems fantasy writers create can have clearly defined rules the reader understands from the get-go, or only certain details are explained. In both cases, the writer will need to remain logically consistent with the details they have revealed. It won't go over well if the rules of magic contradict themselves. In fact, to some readers, it will look like the author didn't spend enough time working out their magic system. Ensure the nuts and bolts are screwed on tightly with your military logistics so the reader can buy in to your world, and then they will be able to easily suspend disbelief of your fantasy and sci-fi elements.

If you want to go down to the fine details about what type of dye and materials are used for the army's banners or the type of timber used in the construction of your civilization's maritime vessels, feel free to do so as, as long as you can work it into another element of story, be it plot, character development, theme, or pacing.

Whatever details you decide on, make sure they are uniquely yours. Adapt the details you find most significant or most interesting for the readers and try to use world-building in military logistics to make it unlike any other story you've read before.

CHAPTER 22

Clothing

For me, personally, one of the most challenging aspects of world-building has always revolved around how to describe the clothing my characters wear. Ever since writing my first novel, I've struggled to convey the image in my mind to the reader.

I think we can all be forgiven for not having a built-up and detailed knowledge of Medieval European, Tang Dynasty, or 23rd-century fashions, and many writers avoid dealing with this problem by using sparse descriptions that do the readers an injustice.

Considering few of us wear fashions from hundreds—sometimes thousands—of years ago, and certainly not fashions from the future, it's not difficult to understand why writers hit a roadblock when they get to this point. Fortunately, it's not all doom and gloom. We can learn about some of the staple garments worn back in the day and also prognosticate fashion trends of the future with a little imagination and scouring of the resources at our disposal.

Whenever I met a roadblock describing the details of an outfit I really wanted to share with my readers, I searched through historical images and even LARP (live action role-playing) photos and clothing vendors on the internet. I'd find an exquisite dress that would give me an idea for my story, but how could I describe those unfamiliar sleeves, a certain pattern of embroidery, or a design I was unfamiliar with?

I still get stumped from time to time, but I do my best. I've certainly gotten a lot of use out of resources like the *Reverse Dictionary*.

In this chapter, we will look at some important garments for not only the noble classes but also the peasantry. I also want to present a couple of staple garments from outside the Western Tradition. Several traditional East Asian garments often appear in fantasy, as does some important traditional African garments. Keep in mind, as I say East Asia and Africa, I'm acknowledging that the details I provide in this chapter are just the tip of the iceberg. More detailed research is recommended to get an accurate picture of the cultures you hope to base part of your fantasy on. I'm no expert on Western fashion, let alone these others, but I wanted to give writers a place to start exploring. I encourage writers to familiarize themselves with foreign cultures and customs previously unfamiliar to them whenever possible.

For English-language writers, Fantasy often harkens back to images of Medieval European culture—especially historical England. Many of us studied western civilization all throughout our public educational experience and were further influenced by popular culture through stories such as *King Arthur*, *The Lord of the Rings*, *A Song of Ice and Fire*, and *The Wheel of Time*, and movies like *Braveheart*, *The NeverEnding Story*, *The Princess Bride*, *Willow*, *The Sword and the Stone*, and *Harry Potter*.

I live and write in China these days (circa 2020) and it's interesting to see a familiar pattern play out in the world of Chinese fantasy. The lion's share of the world-building comes from Chinese Dynastic history—the Tang, Ming, and Qin Dynasties respectfully. Writers take liberty to blend elements and mythology from different time periods, but by and large, they are Chinese-language stories based in part on Chinese history, just as American, European, and other Western writers often base their stories in some part on the culture they've been force-fed from a young age.

That doesn't mean we can't step out of our comfort zone and learn something new. By respecting and highlighting the cultural heritage from different backgrounds, we not only give the readers a more-varied experience, but we also learn a lot. I'm currently working on an epic fantasy series that adapts two large kingdoms, one with Western influence and one with Eastern influence, and I've had a terrific time researching and learning along the way.

I t's important to think about the different socio-economic statuses in the world you are creating. Peasants have less access to valuable resources and have different utilitarian needs than nobles. These facts should factor heavily in the type of clothing and materials used when you are brainstorming wardrobes for your wonderful characters. Let's take a brief look at some examples that I find useful.

A great place to start is with the ubiquitous tunic. A simple garment, worn by both men and women and across socio-economic classes! Tunics were typically worn over underclothing such as a simple shirt and drawers. Even peasants could afford tunics with decorative embroidery or tablet-woven braids.

Tunics had various sleeve-and-hem lengths making them a versatile article of clothing. Often, simple tunics were made from wool or linen, but silk or silk-trimmed tunics were often made for the noble and merchant classes, though those tunics were less common and much more costly.

An example from my novel, *The Inquisitor*.

"They'd dressed him in a long-sleeved cream linen tunic, tan linen trousers, and a lightly tanned leather belt, with a sheepskin cloak as well as fur-lined pantoffles and wool socks."

In this scene, the character goes from being in a dirty dungeon with only the most basic of clothing, to being given nice clothing as he leaves the dungeons to conduct the tasks assigned to him. He makes note of every little article of clothing he's given, right down to the socks, because it's been a long time since he's worn such things.

Doublets are a great item of clothing to add to your world-building, especially if you want to express a measure of extravagance to your readers. Do you remember those gorgeous doublets worn by the psychotic Joffrey Baratheon on the *Game of Thrones* television series? If not, take a look at some picture or video clips online for some examples of absolutely stunning doublets. They scream wealth and privilege.

Doublets are tight-fitted jackets often worn under a gown, mantle, or jerkin and worn with hose that provided ties to hold the garment in place. Doublets were usually decorated with patterns of small cuts in the fabric, embroidery, and braid.

Here's another brief example from *The Inquisitor.*

"He wore a purple velvet doublet with golden trim formed in the shape of a crescent moon and black leather gloves. Nestor pegged him as slightly taller than himself with long, golden hair flowing down around his shoulders. His finely plucked eyebrows and cleanly shaven face gave him a look of one younger than his twenty-six summers and strikingly handsome."

In this case, the character is seeing the son of a powerful nobleman for the first time and sizing him up. I try to use some details on dress and fashion sense to give the reader a clearer image in the hope that they are almost seeing things through my character's eyes.

Jerkins are another common article of clothing that I like adding to certain characters in my stories. Again, for an excellent visual, not enough praise can be given to the costume and wardrobe team on *Game of Thrones*. Characters like Ned Stark, Robb Stark, and Jon Snow wore jerkins on a daily basis.

Jerkins are short, close-fitted men's jackets usually made of light-colored leather and cut sleeveless. Worn over doublets, they often provided protection against slashes in case of a minor skirmish. Soldiers wore a type of jerkin called a buff coat under plate armor.

Men wore cloaks, trousers, leggings, and other accessories. Fur-lined and woolen cloaks were common enough. Cloaks were usually attached by a single brooch made from materials such as bone, horn, thorn, or wood. They could also be tied, laced, or clasped in place.

Belts were a necessity, not a fashion statement for commoners. Other accessories included leather-strapped shoes, hats and hoods, gloves or mittens, gold and silver chains, bracelets of gold, silver, or ivory, and a myriad of fancy brooches.

Peasant women tended to wear tunics with a sleeveless overgarment, with or without a hood, or various manner of dresses. Hoods consisted of either a scarf wrapped around the head and neck or a hooded mantle. Tailored, ankle-length gowns were common, though these garments were sometimes quite extravagant for those with the means. Smocks, hose, kirtles, dresses, belts, surcoats, girdles, capes, and bonnets are all reasonable choices for fantasy attire. Head-dresses, rennin, and veils can also add interesting feeling about your characters if described well.

The most common materials used in many of these articles of clothing included wool, fur, linen, cambric, silk, and cloth of gold or silver—again peasants and nobles would have access to different qualities of fabric. Don't have your farmers sowing the fields in cloth of gold doublets!

Here's an example from *Daughter of Dragons* where the point-of-view character rationalizes why she is wearing clothing that doesn't function well on a physically intensive tromp through the wilds.

"The stifling heat made her regret her choice of clothing. The black silk dress and silver cape weren't especially suitable for a mid-day hike, but as a queen, she didn't have the choice to dress down like others. It was crucial to stand out from the savages of the badlands if you wanted to control them. Hence the gold at her throat, wrist, and finger."

Now, let me introduce a couple of common garments from traditional East Asian garb and from some traditional parts of Africa. If these garments intrigue you, then by all means learn more about the cultures and people surrounding them. It could add a whole other level to your future stories.

One of the most well-known garments of East Asia is the Japanese kimono, a flat, T-shaped garment with square sleeves, worn left over right. The kimono is typically worn with an "obi" —a Japanese sash—and "zori"—flat, thonged wood sandals—and tabi socks. Kimonos are worn by both men and women. As one can imagine after looking at some of the more beautiful and elaborate kimonos, the quality of material would say a lot about the person wearing the kimono.

Lesser known to Westerners is the hakama, a kind of Japanese trousers worn over the lower part of the kimono and tied at the waist. These ankle-length trousers could be both ceremonially formal or functional for daily life. It would be beneficial to add at least two main types of hakama. A hakama with divided leg for horseback riding, and a hakama with undivided leg for daily life or ceremonies. A simple form of hakama could be used for field laborers. This simpler garment would be looser in the waist and narrower in the leg, allowing better movement. The feel of the material might be rough for the cheaper materials, such as wool, and softer for the more costly materials like striped silk.

Hanfu is a traditional style of Chinese clothing that were popular during various periods in Chinese history—especially during the Qin Dynasty—and has even shown some resurgence today among younger Chinese people. Hanfu constitutes too broad a range of garments to cover in this brief introduction, but a standard outfit often included an upper garment such as a silk robe, and a lower garment such as a long skirt, sometimes pleated. Hanfu styles are worn by both men and women.

Upper garments consisted of yi, which fit loosely and open. Lower garments consisted of skirts called chang. Sleeves of Hanfu outfits tend to be long and loose. Sashes are commonly worn to keep the garments secured around the waist. Many colors of silk and intricate embroidery are common.

If you are a writer or reader interested in Chinese historical fantasy, you'll want to delve deeper into Hanfu fashions as they vary tremendously based on a person's position or status.

Historically, very few Chinese people could afford elaborate Hanfu, but Chinese peasants had their own manner of dress. Sometimes called Duan Da, this outfit was made from coarse materials and not smooth silks. These garments also called Shu He, which refers to the woven hemp or animal hair used in the production of the garments. Instead of a long skirt, Duan Da had long, slimmer-fitting trousers, better for doing farm work in a mostly agrarian society and to keep the cloth from snagging on objects while doing daily tasks.

Here are two examples of Asian-inspired world-building with garment descriptions from J.C. Kang's novel *Songs of Insurrection*.

"How was she supposed to sing with the inner robe and gold sash squeezing her chest, in a futile attempt to misrepresent her woefully underdeveloped curves? The tight fold of the skirts concealed her lanky legs, but forced a deliberate pace. At least the short stride delayed the inevitable, while preventing her unsightly feet from tripping on the hanging sleeves of the vermilion outer gown."

What an excellent way to interweave details of the character's wardrobe with her feelings of insecurity and inadequacy to form an interesting scene in which we can sympathize with the character's situation. It's not just detail for detail's sake. It's world-building with a purpose.

Another excellent example is the same character's feelings on seeing her father. "Yellow robes embroidered with auspicious symbols on the chest and elbows hung over his gaunt frame. Gone was the robust optimism she remembered from her childhood."

Again, the minor clothing descriptions are blended to create an impression of the character's father, contrasting with her memories of him from better times. It feels natural and seamless.

In some parts of Africa, the kanzu is a popular traditional article of clothing. White or cream in color, and worn by men, the kanzu is ankle-length pants made from a myriad of fabrics including barkcloth, silk, cotton, poplin, or linen. Maroon embroidery around the collar, abdomen, and sleeves are common.

The gomesi is a brightly colored floor-length dress with a square neckline, short, puffed sleeves, and tied with a sash below the waist. These garments are made of expensive silk, cotton, or linen. Gomesi are worn by women in several African countries and are famous for their beauty and intricate patterns.

Adding elements from traditional African cultures is a great way to diversify your world and represent different groups of people and interesting aspects of culture you might miss out on if you stick to only Western tropes.

CHAPTER 23

Armor

Think of armor as protective battle clothing because that's what it is. Armor comes in many shapes and sizes, but its functionality and affordability determined what type of it that people wore. Of course, nobles and castle guards sometimes wore ceremonial armor that lacked the functionality of armor on the battlefield, but the majority of armor served the explicit purpose of protecting the wearer from bodily harm in combat.

Let's start with shields. A shield is a form of hand-held armor that can also be strapped to the forearm. Shields were commonly used to protect the wearer from slashes or stabs from edged and pointed weapons, specifically swords, spears, and arrows. Shields varied greatly in shape and size depending on their function and the weapon they were partnered with.

Early shields were made from solid wood, wicker, reeds, and animal hide. Later, shields were crafted from several different metals like bronze and steel.

In my own writing, I've failed miserably to include enough shields. Shields have been essential in combat from times of antiquity. A sword and shield made for a formidable pair.

Aside from a boomerang comic book shield, few shields gain much notoriety in fantasy and sci-fi mediums. An iconic shield from the realm of video games was certainly the Hylian Shield used by the Knights of Hyrule and by the hero Link in the *Legend of Zelda* franchise. The Hylian Shield bears the symbol of the Triforce and the red Hylian crest. These shields were steel but lightweight and couldn't burn like the more common wooden shields.

Speaking of which, it's a great touch to have your less than wealthy fighters making do with wooden shields as those would be by far the most common type of shield. Not everyone can purchase a sword, either! As you read the section on weapons, consider what weapons someone in your character's economic class might have access to before giving them a katana just because it's a cool Japanese sword and you are writing an Asian-inspired fantasy.

Chainmail—also known just as mail— is armor made from hundreds of metal rings linked together into a protective mesh. A full coat of chainmail is called a hauberk. In fantasy, scale armor is a popular armor with a similar construction but with beautiful and durable dragon scale instead of metal rings.

As with most metal armor, chainmail was costly to purchase and time-consuming to craft, but it gave a fighter a huge advantage over others in combat as the wearer could survive otherwise dismembering or penetrating injuries with no more than bruising.

The Roman Empire introduced chainmail to Asia and the Middle East. The technology passed into Central Asia and was eventually introduced to China and Japan.

Chainmail would have been an excellent choice to protect against edged and piercing weapons. The most common crafting pattern in Europe was a four-to-one pattern. Each ring was linked to four others. Mail tended to be crafted from wrought iron or heat-treated steel.

❄

Here is an example from *Daughter of Dragons* where I use chainmail to express world-building.

"Captain Herzi led Laurena into the room. The walls were lined with wooden racks. Along the sidewalls were polished helms, steel shin guards, gauntlets, and a few sets of hapoi chainmail. The mail would be worth a fortune on the open market. Along the back wall, the racks were full of breastplates, some painted a regal gold, others the natural steel."

The suits of armor we always see in museums or at jousting events in films that seems to cover every inch of the fighter's body is plate armor, made from bronze, iron, or steel plates. This style of armor was especially useful for heavy cavalry. It allowed a soldier and his plate-covered war horse to charge through the enemy lines, causing havoc in a battle. Plate armor was also quite heavy, so allowing the horse to carry the weight was ideal, but foot soldiers and nobles also wore plate armor.

In Japan, iron plate cuirasses and helmets were already skillfully crafted as early as the Kofun Period. Different regions produced plate armor with different characteristics.

Here is an in-depth example of armor description from Joseph Malik's second novel *The New Magic*.

"Javal's traveling armor was a long black shirt of heavy-gauge mail slitted up the crotch for riding, with twin gold braids—four-ragères—designating his rank tied through his mail at his shoulder and looped under his right arm. His helmet, also black, had a hinged visor slitted for his eyes. He wore it open so that the rain dripped off it into a leather gorget and mantle and a thick fur cape over his shoulder."

Malik goes deep on the descriptive elements to provide a hard-fantasy image for the reader. The level of realism and research involved makes a pact with the reader, promising authenticity within the world-building.

Protective helmets—also called helms—were an essential part of historical armor. Enclosed helmets were commonly worn over a mail coif and had head-padding inside to cushion the head.

In China, bronze helmets, leather armor, and breastplates made of shell were crafted as early as the Shang Dynasty. By the time of the Warring States Period, helmets were refined with stream-lined styles suitable to deflect glancing blows from weapons, increasing a combatant's chances of survival in warfare.

In sci-fi, most helmets are part of spacesuits that provide oxygen or for aliens to sustain other forms of life support. In Robert Heinlein's *Starship Troopers*, the space marines wear an armored spacesuit and helmet for combat with the Arachnids—an alien species of insectoids. Sleek and functional, these spacesuits and helmets have a realism that is impressive for a fifty-year-old novel.

In the *Metroid video* game franchise, the heroine Samus Aran wears a special type of armor and helmet called the Power Suit. This suit can incorporate upgrades and absorb heavy damage while also sustaining life-support systems in hostile envi-ronments. Her helmet looks similar to that of an astronaut's, allowing her to see a wide view of her surroundings—unlike the narrow slits that protected the eyes on medieval helmets.

In fiction, helmets sometimes hide the face and create a feeling of mystery. Many villains have helmets designed to look like the open maw of a dragon, lion, or wolf to scare their foes, but it also reveals something about the warrior who wears it to the reader—think of the character Sandor Clegane, known as the Hound from *A Song of Ice and Fire* with his helm of a vicious dog's head.

Each time the Hound is described in the books, a stronger image of the character develops. Some of that has to do with the descriptions of his helmet, weapons, and physical characteristics.

WRITING TIP: Figure out which kind of characters are most likely to wear which type of armor. Better yet, give their armor a personal touch—like we read in this chapter, from Malik's *The New Magic*. Be conscious that giving each important character realistic and personal descriptions, whether that be of weapons, armor, physical appearance, or anything else helps the character stick firmly within the reader's mind so they aren't thinking "Who is this character?" again in the next chapter.

CHAPTER 24

Weapons

There are so many different types of weapons in science fiction and fantasy, you might wonder if we are a wee bit too enamored with fighting each other. More likely, you wouldn't spend a second thought on the idea, instead finding yourself interested in the choice of weapons used by a particular character or the capabilities of the weapons—especially in the case of sci-fi weapons.

There are more than enough weapons in these two genres to write several lengthy tomes and still just scratch the surface of their world-building potential. Instead, we'll look at some of the most commonly used weapons and—in the case of sci-fi—a couple of the more interesting if uncommon ones.

Remember, some resources are available in the appendix of this book for writers who want a bit of direction on where to look next for more information. I've tried to include references to everything I've studied while writing this book, so I trust everyone will find something of value to dive deeper down the rabbit hole.

As for me, I recently found myself researching more on swords and how they are forged. The new knowledge I've gained has made it a lot more fun to write about weapons with the breadth and depth it demands.

In science fiction, weapons range from handheld devices like phasers all the way up the scale to weapons of mass destruction like star destroyers and other doomsday devices.

The classic sci-fi weapon is undoubtedly the ray gun. A staple of B-movie posters for many years, the ray gun represented the imaginative leap from firearms to something less crude and even more powerful. Ray guns were great for old movies because they could have a scene with the camera focused on the hero shooting his ray gun and then cut over to the villain's remains—a smoking pile of charred bits. No death-scene acting required.

When a reader is shown a ray gun early in a story, they know they are likely to see more amazing technology. It's a taste of things to come, which is a great use of world-building.

Over time, the phaser replaced the ray gun. The *Star Trek* franchise popularized the phaser—which is not a ray or laser like sci-fi weapons of the past had been based on—but particles fired by way of a plasma beam (sounds so cool and techy!). The beam also features a key technology—adjustable levels of lethal and non-lethal intensity. In poorly done sci-fi, this results in a plot device with the gun on stun or kill modes as needed, but often a fancy way to knock a character out for some length of time. There was often no explanation on how a phaser achieved a knockout. I don't think it's clear to the average reader how a plasma stream makes someone lose consciousness without causing serious permanent damage. Try to avoid using your phasers or other weapons so poorly in your own writing.

I n *Star Trek*, the phaser had interesting uses beyond harming foes. If an away team found themselves in a harsh and cold environment with no way to beam off planet, they could use their phaser to heat to act as an impromptu heater for the crew. This was always my favorite use of the phaser because it made it feel like a Swiss Army knife instead of just a sidearm. It had me wondering what other clever uses could be made of the plasma beam.

Phasers are a sleeker, cleaner gun. There's no smoke or powder from the shot, no loud noise, no messy discarded casings or nasty bullet holes. You either missed, stunned, or killed your enemy. But it did still represent the weapon at the warrior's side ready to be used as necessary, but less savage than a sword, an axe, or even a six-shooter.

The phaser was also a world-building element of a particular faction in the universe. The Federation and, more specifically, Star Fleet used the phaser as their go-to weapon. Ask yourself who uses the special weapons in the universes you create. What does it say about those groups? How does it give them a sense of agency or differentiation from other factions?

Writing Tip: Allow the choice of weapons by each faction in your universe to help tell the story of who they are and what they value. Not all future factions in science fiction employ phasers, as we all know.

On the stranger and more exotic side, I've always been intrigued by nanotechnology and the chilling possibilities of weaponizing it. The first nanotech novel I read that really left a deep impact on me was Michael Crichton's Prey. *Prey* is a goose-bump-inducing techno thriller in which a swarm of nanobots have somehow developed a type of hive-mind intelligence and what danger they pose to the whole of society.

The story is clearly in the vein of "What if science goes too far?" as many of Crichton's books, such as *Jurassic Park*, asks. That's where the stories derive a certain page-turning mystical quality, capturing our imagination and asking us terrifying questions.

Nanobots pose a serious threat if weaponized because their size makes them difficult to stop or even to detect. A writer could use them to spy, to infect, to sabotage. Using nano weapons also allows you to think about potential countermeasures to such threats. How could a faction defend themselves from such weapons? Your weapons give you the opportunity to create defenses. The more believable your weapons and defenses are, the more your readers will sink deeper into your story.

Sentient weapons are another category to be familiar with. Take the *Terminator* franchise, for example. This sci-fi portal thriller is about a sentient robot assassin from the future that has traveled back in time to murder an important person. The protagonists need to use contemporary weapons to fight against the advanced technology of the T-100 and, in later installments, liquid metal and even nanotech terminators.

Sentient weapons are interesting because they give the writer a chance to decide whether robots will have a certain degree of agency and self-discovery or whether they will be instruments of brutal efficiency. The T-100 only has one objective defined in its parameters—to eliminate Sarah Connor. In this way, the robot feels cold. As is told to us by Sarah Connor's protector Kyle Reese, the terminator can't be bargained with. That creates a zero-sum tension in which the story will build until a final encounter where the machine either accomplishes its mission or fails—allowing our hero to live another day . . . until the next machine is sent back in time after her.

Ridley Scott goes a different way in *Blade Runner*. The dystopian film uses androids to ask questions about what it means to be human. How much agency do these androids have? Are we somehow more real than they are? Do we deserve the right to give them expiration dates?

While some of the androids in *Blade Runner* give us a reason to hate them, namely by killing people, others are just trying to live their lives like any other human would—laying low from those that would seek to control them for as long as they can.

So, whichever route you take, be it the self-aware machine gun or the self-reflecting replicant, use this weapon in the broader context of world-building to say something thematic about the characters, places, and story you have created.

These are just a few starting paths a writer could take with science-fiction weaponry.

In high fantasy, we often have cruder weapons, objects our ancestors used like the sword, bow and arrow, the spear, and the war hammer.

The sword is the most iconic of historic and fantasy weapons and is featured prominently in stories from all over the world.

Many memorable swords can be found in fantasy novels. For example, in *ASOIAF*, the Stark family's two-handed greatsword Ice is heavily featured in several different plot points of the story, and what happens to Ice has meaning that can be felt by the reader.

J.R.R. Tolkien created several memorable swords, including Sting and Anduril, to name just a few. Sting has a great story; forged by the elves as a short sword, it was the perfect size for a small hobbit like Bilbo Baggins, and he carried it with him as his token item until he got a hold of the One Ring. Sting was no mere sword, though. Tolkien included aspects of his world-building, making the sword possess magical properties. The sword would glow bright blue whenever goblins or orcs approached. This tells us that elves have had problems with these creatures for a very long time and foreshadows that later in the book the sword will glow bright blue and there'll be trouble to deal with.

Anduril was forged from the shards of another legendary sword Narsil. The elves enchanted the sword to prevent it from breaking or staining and gave Anduril to Aragon. He was able to control a huge ghost army near the end of the trilogy with the help of Anduril, and it played into the lore of the story because it scared Sauron when he saw Narsil reforged into Anduril.

I n Dustin Porta's novel *Whalemoon*, a rapier once called the Blade of Bosun Lee—once wielded by the world's greatest duelist—became cursed after the duelist used it to take his own life. The curse was that anyone who wields the sword will win their battle but die before they can sheath the Blade of Bosun Lee.

This makes the sword at once powerful and so dangerous one would have to be crazy—or in a really tough spot. Porta has created a magic system in his story based on folklore and bloodshed, both of which factor into the lore and mystery surrounding this sword and other weapons and magical objects in *Whalemoon*.

Another unique example comes from Brandon Sanderson's *Stormlight Archive*. Shardblades are known for slicing through solid rock and severing souls from their bodies. The only physical sign that the shard blade has harmed someone is that the victim's eyes burn out. Each Shardblade is unique and come from a much older type of weapon called Honorblades. The blades must also be summoned. The wielder wills them into existence, and this process is said to take ten heartbeats. As with much of Sanderson's world-building, the blades have a deep history and many properties that blend seamlessly within his world.

Besides blades, there are other iconic weapons in fantasy like the bow and arrow. My favorite example comes from the *Legend of Zelda* franchise. The wizard princess Zelda wields the Bow of Light and the Light Arrows throughout much of the series of video games and stories. Zelda does not wear a quiver leading many to speculate that the Bow of Light makes the powerful Light Arrows magically. Light Arrows travel through their targets and are more powerful than normal arrows. Princess Zelda also uses them to control powerful phantoms which is a magical property bestowed upon the arrows.

One of the reasons I really liked these magical items was that they belonged to the mysterious Princess Zelda. Back then, we didn't have many women represented in a hero's role. Granted, early on, Zelda was used as a damsel in distress, but she evolved steadily into a powerful character with a level of agency.

If you decide to use a special bow and arrow, be careful not to go the derivative elves-with-arrows route. It pins you into a worldbuilding corner, forcing you to give the readers a good reason for not giving the bow to someone else.

Writing about combat is a technical matter and requires making some conscious decisions. If you decide to give a blow-by-blow account, you need to be familiar with the terminology, the mechanics, and the techniques of fighting with a given weapon. If that scares you, it's often better to leave much of the battle to the imagination with phrases similar to "The clashing of their blades echoed through the night as the two swordsmen tried to gain the upper hand . . ."

It's hard to write interesting blow-by-blow fight scenes. They lack the visual appeal of a choreographed fight scene from the movies, but don't be afraid to describe a key strike, parry, or slash that advances the fight or leads to the end of it.

Consider adding weapons featured less in fantasy novels—warhammers, spears, and throwing daggers. My favorite warhammer lore takes place in the world of *ASOIAF*. In book one —*A Game of Thrones*—King Robert Baratheon is past his prime fighting years but talks nostalgically about fighting with his mighty warhammer.

You see, during Robert's Rebellion, the young Baratheon led a force alongside Ned Stark, Jon Arryn, and others. I've already spoken of the backstory in the chapter on building a history, but the war came down to an epic showdown at the Battle of the Trident. Prince Rhaegar Targaryen and Robert Baratheon met in single combat with the battle fought by the two armies around them. After being wounded by Prince Rhaegar, Robert Baratheon buried his warhammer in Prince Rhaegar's chest, killing him and effectively turning the tide of the war.

Ned Stark—a great fighter in his own right—could not wield Robert's warhammer even with two hands, but Robert Baratheon could swing it with one hand, which speaks to the power and skill of the man. It was the stuff legends are made of for the future king of the Seven Kingdoms.

Weapons should help the writer tell the story. The more integrated the character's main weapon is to the backstory, world-building, and character-development, the better.

❄

CHAPTER 25

Fantastic Beasts

Wondrous creatures and unique aliens make up some of the most important aspects of world-building. In the epic fantasy genre, you can hardly call your work fantasy without a mythical creature showing up every once in a while to remind the reader that they are exploring a place unlike Earth, unlike their daily experiences.

In sci-fi, what's more intriguing than the crew of an exploration vessel making contact with a new alien life form? I remember so many episodes of *Star Trek* where I'd get the chance to see futuristic humans interacting with other peer-level species like Klingons and Vulcans and the interesting interactions with life forms like the Borg and the Q.

Dragons are part of the psyche of fantasy readers and are almost compulsory in epic fantasy. Unicorns have gained status as a creature with more symbolism than substance. It's not difficult for a unicorn to turn into a McGuffin because it's often more symbolically important than as a living, unique creature with a mind of its own.

In outer space, on a strange new world, the writer is free to imagine new life forms in an almost unrestrained manner. As long as the creature fits the environment and story, the sky is the limit!

There are more expectations from fantasy readers on what particular fantastic beasts are in the books they read. Some readers want dragons, period. Others are lovers of everything Fae and want to see faerie tropes play out across different stories. Reader expectations are important to manage, but the writer certainly has room to throw in other mythical creatures that fit the story and lead in interesting directions.

I n *Daughter of Dragons*, I introduce a manticore in the flashback prologue, and I bring that creature back into the story, in what I hope is an interesting way, near the end of the epic.

"Long wings stirred up a billow of dust from the dry floor of the ravine as the creature landed on the far side of the creek. Its fur was red as blood with a mane flowing like the fires of Mount Dumoria. A long tail curved over the creature's back, its shiny stinger glimmering from the light off the water of the shallow creek.

'Your Grace.'

The tremors had left Sorceress Yali's voice and she sounded more composed. 'What manner of lion is *that*?'

'That's no lion. That's a blood manticore . . ."

Try to set a scene in a location that will highlight the uniqueness of the creature you want to share with the reader. Use details or actions to highlight how the creature is different from what the characters are used to or how it's different than other beasts.

The most well-known fantasy creature is surely the dragon. Stories dating back thousands of years speak of these fearsome monsters. And hardly a book cover in the epic fantasy genre can pass quality control without a dragon somewhere in the art, even if there are no dragons in the story.

Western dragons are symbolic of man's greed, lust, and personal weaknesses. Ask yourself why a dragon feels the need to covet riches and virgins. In later years, many writers have tried to make this a shiny-object thing and ditched the virgin-napping, but the fact remains, slaying a dragon is akin to killing the bad parts of yourself. In contemporary stories, dragons are almost as likely to be an ally as an enemy.

I first became really enamored with dragons by reading the *Dragonlance Chronicles* as a young boy. That series made an effort to incorporate a lot of interesting dragons and sort of opened the door for writers to continue experimenting with dragons.

In the East, there are dragons of a completely different variety. Eastern dragons are associated with good fortune and tend to have powers over the weather and the seas. Eastern dragons are almost never evil. Some of the earlier examples of dragons in Chinese literature come from the compilation of mythologies in *Classic of Mountains and Seas.* This collection of stories was written by many hands over many centuries. For a more contemporary and completely different example of dragons, I recommend checking out the English translation of *Heavy-Sweetness Ash-like Frost* by Dian Xian. This fantasy romance features a shifting water dragon that spends a lot of his time as a good-looking dude. The story is well done and was even made into a television series that was featured on Netflix.

I've included a dragon worshipped like a goddess and a baby dragon that tags along with my young protagonist, and I certainly take notice that readers often mention the dragons when they ask me about my books. In *The Buried Giant*, Kazuo Ishiguro uses a giant largely as a Mcguffin, which somehow seems to work; perhaps because it was literary fiction, but it was certainly a unique way to incorporate a dragon into his fantasy.

Another creature seemingly more and more popular by the year is the faerie. Faeries are typically presented as magical, flying, pranksters. Often female or non-gendered, faeries flutter about through enchanted forests, sometimes letting their curiosity get the better of them. They are often introduced in epic fantasy as side characters who help the protagonist along their quest when they've hit a rough spot, or they help the protagonists learn something through pacifying them with a spell or charm. Often depicted with wings like butterflies or even like leaves, Disney— through the popularity of the classic cartoon *Peter Pan*—introduced Tinkerbell who had a huge influence on the popularity and direction of faeries in fantasy.

Unicorns and pegasi are common inclusions to consider for your works. Unicorns represent rarity and purity in modern fantasy, and many older stories involve virgins taming unicorns. Unicorns harken to the wild beauty of the world. Occasionally, unicorns are used as a "cool horse" trope, which is certainly useful, but a bit shallow and lacking the depth a magical creature should add to your story. Making your hero's pegasus into a personal jet of sorts is certainly the lower bounds of what one can do with a creature as unique as a magical flying horse. In Gaiman's *Stardust*, the protagonist walks into a literal retelling of the Lion and the Unicorn in a fight to the death. Reading the unicorn fighting a savage lion is quite different from the timid gentle unicorns I remember from more innocent fairy tales.

Mermaids and sea monsters are core additions to sea adventures and can make a fantasy really come to life. The sea, in its vastness, holds mysteries that have captivated us since the dawn of time. Mermaids, merfolk, merpeople—whatever you want to call them —are sea-living creatures, sometimes half-human and half-fish, or sometimes with both humanoid and fish characteristics blended together. Chinese medieval writing even has several references to mermaids that cry pearls! In most stories with mermaids, a human male will invariably become romantically involved with a beautiful mermaid.

Sea monsters tend to be larger-than-life dangerous creatures primarily concerned with sinking ships and eating people. Giant squids and indistinct leviathans are the most common portrayals of sea monsters. These creatures are a good world-building device as they emphasize the danger and mystery of the open ocean, and more broadly, the unexplored world. The part of the map yet to be filled in.

Goblins, trolls, and orcs make up a class of creatures that are part of what I consider the most undesirable way to world-build the beasts of a fantasy world. This wildly derivative use of "ugly, green, bad things"—for lack of a better umbrella term— is the most visible form of lazy world-building that I've already spoken of briefly in the previous chapter on one-dimensional races.

These creatures are inserted into the world as an inherently evil and adversarial force, often without their own agency because they are commanded by an even bigger and more powerful baddie. Orcs have rarely been point-of-view characters and are invariably push-over foils for the protagonists to either defeat in combat or outsmart on their way to completing their quest.

If you feel the need to include "ugly, green bad things" into your fantasy, consider a new take on them. Perhaps one is a hero, and clever, and attractive (or is that a bridge too far after how many grotesque interpretations?)

In science fiction, aliens are a key element and easily one of the most intriguing. Who isn't interesting in seeing how a writer will present an alien species to the reader?

Space is vast. Filling it with interesting beings simply makes sense.

Some stories employ the trope of space as an ocean and include things like literal space whales and other such massive sea creatures who have somehow adapted to the extremes of the vacuum of space.

In Terry Pratchett's *The Dark Side of the Sun*, huge beasts called sundogs live out in space. Oddly enough, they aren't aggressive and actually work together with humans. Another example from *Titan A.E.* is the space stingrays, and in *Andromeda* the Cetus is a great brightly-glowing creature resembling a whale, except it eats all types of matter—even planets! Using the theme of the gigantic in space can be an interesting angle.

In my opinion, the most interesting inclusion is of intelligent yet cryptic alien life forms, such as the heptapods in the film *Arrival*. Both familiar and mysterious, these seemingly benevolent aliens were the main draw for me. Of course, on the other end of the spectrum, the xenomorphs from the *Aliens* franchise are so terrifying you want to look away . . . if only you could!

Writing Tip: When choosing an alien species, ask yourself why it must be this type of creature and not another. What is special enough about the concept you have created? Has it been done before? Is it too derivative? In what ways can you make this creature concept unique and therefore necessary for the story?

Author's Note

Over the course of this book, I've tried my best to provide relevant and interesting examples of world-building from many mediums to help you find the best ways to connect with readers. Though we might all be writers, hearing an example from your favorite television show or from a comic book you read as a kid could lead to breakthroughs and deep impressions I wouldn't want to deny anyone.

Many of our top world-building examples come from novels because the imagination knows no bounds. While movies are becoming more and more extraordinary with each passing year, the medium will always be limited by their budgets. And while novels are still limited in their world-building by the restraints of pacing, plot, and character development, what's written within those pages has little to limit the writer except for their experiences and their imagination.

As long as you can find pure joy in creating your world, you're likely to be successful. If you love what you create and are confident in your methods, there is nothing you can't accomplish as a writer.

-H.C. Harrington
November 2020

WHAT'S NEXT?

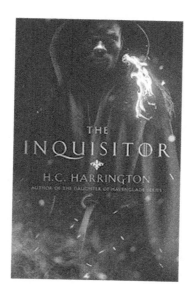

A stand-alone murder mystery novel in the Havenglade world awaits you. The Inquisitor.

A brutal murder, a disgraced inquisitor, and a city of secrets.

From the Amazon best-selling author of Daughter of Havenglade comes, The Inquisitor.

In the port city of Pax Grati, a highborn daughter betrothed to the son of a powerful lord has been brutally murdered.

Nestor Atius, left to rot in the dungeons, has one chance to find the killer and bring justice to her family and the realm.

But when an unlikely friend reveals the investigation is more than meets the eye, Nestor must make a choice.

As he uncovers the truth, it becomes more and more clear, he is the killer's next target.

The Inquisitor

A fantasy mystery from the Havenglade World.

DAUGHTER OF HAVENGLADE ON AUDIOBOOKS!

If you enjoyed the Daughter of Havenglade series you might be interested to know all four books are available in audiobook form narrated by the talented **Kira Grace**.

Try Daughter of Havenglade or give it as a gift to an audiobook listener!

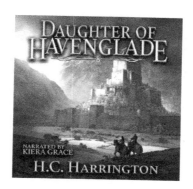

REVIEWS FOR AMAZON AND GOODREADS

Did you enjoy World-Building for Writers?

Amazon and **Goodreads** reviews are the best way for me to get word out about my series and I'd be absolutely honored to receive a review from you today. This is my most effective tool for growing the series my brand and getting closer to creating more of the Havenglade universe that my fans enjoy diving into.

Let Your Voice Be Heard.

Works Referenced

I've provided a simple—yet semi-exhaustive—list of the main works referenced throughout this work and some books I read through during my research, even if they weren't referenced in the final draft. I encourage readers to check out some of these great works if they have the opportunity. I've bolded the authors' surnames for ease of search.

Enjoy!

Frank **Herbert**, *Dune* (1965)

J.R.R. **Tolkien**, *Lord of the Rings, The* (1954), and *The Hobbit* (1937), and *Fellowship of the Ring, The* (1954)

George R.R. **Martin**, *Song of Ice and Fire, A* (1996), *Game of Thrones, A* (1996)

Douglas **Adams**, *Hitchhiker's Guide to the Galaxy, The* (1979)

C.S. **Lewis**, *Chronicles of Narnia, The* (1950)

Piers **Anthony**, *Spell for Chameleon, A* (1977), and *Ogre, Ogre* (1982)

. . .

Margaret **Weis** and Tracy **Hickman**, *Dragonlance Chronicles* (1984), *Dragons of Winter Night* (1985)

Michael **Crichton**, *Jurassic Park* (1990), *Sphere* (1987), *Rising Sun* (1992), and Prey (2002)

Stephen **King**, *Stand, The* (1978), *Shining, The* (1977), Eyes of the Dragon, The (1984), *Pet Semetary* (1983), Dark Tower series, *The* (1982), and *11/22/63* (2011)

Orson Scott **Card**, *Ender's Game* (1985)

Isaac **Asimov**, *Foundation series, The* (1951), *I, Robot* (1950), *Prelude to Foundation* (1988), *Foundation and Empire* (1952), and *Evitable Conflict, The* (1950)

Joseph **Campbell**, *The Hero with a Thousand Faces* (1949), and Bill **Moyers**, *The Power of Myth* (1988), *Masks of God series* (1959)

Philip K. **Dick**, *Do Androids Dream of Electric Sheep?* (1968)

Ursula K. **Le Guin**, *Left Hand of Darkness, The* (1969)

Tom **Pollock**, *Skyscraper Throne series, The* (2012)

. . .

P hilip **Pullman**, *His Dark Materials series* (2000)

R obert **Heinlein**, *Stranger in a Strange Land* (1961), *Starship Troopers* (1959)

R oger **Zelazny**, *Lord of Light* (1967)

M ichael **Ende**, *Neverending Story, The* (1979)

I an **Douglas**, *Heritage series, The* (1998)

L . Frank **Baum**, *Wonderful Wizard of Oz, The* (1900)

F . Scott **Fitzgerald**, *Great Gatsby, The* (1925)

T odd **McFarlane**, *Spawn* (1992)

H .G. **Wells**, *Time Machine, The* (1895), *War of the Worlds, The* (1898)

L iu, Ci Xin, *Three-Body Problem, The* (2008), *Death's End* (2010)

.   .   .

Ari **Bach**, *Valhalla* (2010)

Jim **Butcher**, *Dresden Files, The* (2000)

Patricia **Briggs**, *Mercy Thompson series, The* (2006)

Cassandra **Clare**, *Mortal Instruments series, The* (2014)

Clifton **Hillegrass**, *CliffsNotes* (1958)

J.R. **Ward**, *Blade Dagger Brotherhood* (2015)

Stephenie **Meyer**, *Twilight Saga, The* (2005)

Jeaniene **Frost**, *Night Huntress series, The* (2007)

Gail **Carriger**, *Parasol Protectorate, The* (2009)

Scott **Westerfeld**, *Leviathan series, The* (2009)

. . .

Cherie **Priest**, *Boneshaker* (2009)

Neal **Stephenson**, *Snow Crash* (1992)

J.K. **Rowling**, *Harry Potter series*, (1997)

Laini **Taylor**, *Daughter of Smoke and Bone series* (2011)

Robert **Jordan**, *Wheel of Time series, The* (1990), *Eye of the World, The* (1990)

Brandon **Sanderson**, *Mistborn series* (2006), *Stormlight Archive, The* (2010)

Neil **Gaiman**, *Stardust* (1997), *Sandman, The* (1991)

Erin **Morgenstein**, *Night Circus, The* (2011)

Patrick **Rothfuss**, *Kingkiller Chronicles, The* (2007)

Gabriel Garcia **Marquez**, *One Hundred Years of Solitude* (1967)

. . .

Anne **Rice**, *Vampire Chronicles, The* (1976)

Marc **Okrand**, *Klingon Dictionary, The* (1985)

Carl **Sagan**, *Contact* (1985)

Terry **Pratchett**, *Dark Side of the Sun, The* (1976)

Joseph **Malik**, *Dragon's Trail* (2016), *New Magic, The* (2018)

J.C. **Kang**, *Thorn of the Night Blossoms* (2019), *Songs of Insurrection* (2017)

William **Gibson**, *Johnny Mnemonic* (1981), *Neuromancer* (1984)

Arthur C. **Clarke**, *2001: Space Odyssey, A* (1968)

David J. **Peterson**, *Art of Language Invention, The* (2015)

Kazuo **Ishiguro**, *Buried Giant, The* (2015)

. . .

Unknown, *Classic of Mountains and Seas* (unknown)

Dian Xian, *Heavy-Sweetness Ash-like Frost* (2014)

Dustin **Porta**, *Whalemoon* (2019)

Wizards RPG Team, *Players Handbook. 5Th Ed. D&D* (2014), *Dungeon Master's Guide 5th Ed.* (2014), *Monstrous Compendium, The* (1989)

Bantam Books, *Choose Your Own Adventure series* (1979)

James Fenimore **Cooper**, *Last of the Mohicans, The* (1826)

Mark **Rosenfelder**, *Language Construction Kit, The* (2010)

H.C. **Harrington**, *Daughter of Havenglade* (2016), *Black Dragon Deceivers* (2017), *Blood Cauldron* (2018), *Daughter of Dragons* (2019), *Inquisitor, the* (2019), *Havenglade Tales* (2020)

FILM AND WEBSITE REFERENCES

Lucasfilm, *Star Wars Universe, The* (1978), *Return of the Jedi* (1983), *A New Hope* (1977)

Gene **Roddenberry**, *Star Trek Universe, The* (1966), *Andromeda* (2000)

Universal Pictures, *Waterworld* (1995)

George **Miller**, *Mad Max* (1979)

William **Hjortsberg**, Legend (1985)

Ridley **Scott**, *Alien* (1979) *Blade Runner* (1982)

Jim **Henson**, *Dark Crystal, The* (1982), *Dark Crystal: Age of Resistance, The (2019)*

Disney, *Ferngully* (1992), *Pocahontas (1995), Peter Pan (1953)*

James **Cameron**, *Avatar* (2009) *Terminator, the* (1984)

Fox Animation Studios, *Titan A.E.* (2000)

Paramount Pictures, *Event Horizon* (1997), *Arrival* (2016)

Dean **Devlin**, Roland **Emmerich**, *Star Gate* (1994)

Warner Bros., *Wild Wild West* (1999), *Blade Runner* (1982)

Robert K. **Weiss** and Tracy **Torme**, *Sliders* (1995)

HBO, *Game of Thrones* (2011)

Marvel Comics, *Blade series* (1998)

Nintendo, *Legend of Zelda, The* (1986)

lotr.fandom.com/wiki/miruvor

glyphweb.com/arda/m/miruvor.php

startrek.com/database_article/gagh

Gameofthrones.fandom.com/wiki/food_and_drink
One of my favorite word-building webpages.

https://gameofthrones.fandom.com/wiki/Armament

hitchhikers.fandom.com/wiki/ pan_galactic_gargle_blaster

Daughterofhavenglade.com
The website for my *Daughter of Havenglade* Epic Fantasy series.

http://en.wikipedia.org/wiki/melange_(fictional_drug)

https://www.kboards.com/index.php/board,60.0.html
A great resource to network with indie authors on a host of topics.

https://tvtropes.org/
Some specific searches on tropes discussed within this book are *green skinned space babe, not quite human, crystal dragon Jesus, used future, shiny looking spaceships, science fiction, doomsday device, cyber punk, steampunk, ray gun, space opera,* and *burial in space.* To name a few.

https://www.youtube.com/watch?v=ATN
A great world-building lecture by Brandon Sanderson.

www.duolingo.com

A free language learning application which I reference in the book. They offer a full course on High Valyrian as well as many other languages constructed or otherwise.

https://reversedictionary.org/

One of the best "what's the right word?" resources on the net.

https://learnnavi.com

https://en.wikipedia.org/wiki/Constructed_language

I've included a number of Wikipedia entries as starting points for many of the examples I've used throughout this book. Here are some sample pages you might find useful.

https://en.wikipedia.org/wiki/Na'vi_language

https://en.wikipedia.org/wiki/Black_Speech

https://en.wikipedia.org/wiki/Valyrian_languages#High_Valyrian

https://en.wikipedia.org/wiki/Dothraki_language

https://en.wikipedia.org/wiki/Shield

https://en.wikipedia.org/wiki/Verb-initial_word_order

https://en.wikipedia.org/wiki/Trireme

https://en.wikipedia.org/wiki/Gomesi

https://en.wikipedia.org/wiki/Kanzu

https://en.wikipedia.org/wiki/Tunic

https://en.wikipedia.org/wiki/Doublet_(clothing)

https://en.wikipedia.org/wiki/English_medieval_clothing

https://en.wikipedia.org/wiki/Ancient_Chinese_clothing

https://en.wikipedia.org/wiki/Chain_mail

https://www.sfwa.org/2019/08/09/military-logistics-for-fantasy-writers/

A great article on military logistics and world-building.

https://inkarnate.com/

An excellent resource for mapmaking.

https://www.artstation.com/community/channels?sort_by=community

An interesting resource for finding inspiration.

worldbuilding.stackexchange.com

ABOUT THE AUTHOR

H.C. Harrington is an American novelist, teacher, and lifetime learner. From Orange County, Ca. he studied Anthropology and History receiving his degree from the University of Nevada. He is the author of the Amazon #1 Best-Selling Daughter of Havenglade Fantasy Series, as well as the Fantasy Murder-Mystery The Inquisitor.

After setting aside archaeological digs in the Sierra Nevadas, H.C. moved to Chengdu, China to study Mandarin Chinese. During his writing journey, he has lived and traveled to more than a dozen countries.

His hobbies include traveling, playing boardgames, creating constructed languages, backpacking, and reading.

For more information or to contact him directly, visit daughterofhavenglade.com

You can also get notices for his new releases delivered right to your in-box by joining his newsletter or by following him on any of the social media links below. Follow H.C. Harrington on Bookbub.

Made in the USA
Middletown, DE
26 September 2023